JK
1341   Hacker
.H2   Congressional
1964   districting

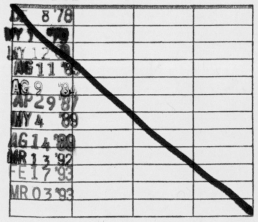

CONGRESSIONAL DISTRICTING
The Issue of Equal Representation

CONGRESSIONAL DISTRICTING

The Issue of Equal Representation

By

Andrew Hacker

Revised Edition

The Brookings Institution · *Washington, D.C.*

THE BROOKINGS INSTITUTION is an independent organization devoted to nonpartisan research, education, and publication in economics, government, foreign policy, and the social sciences generally. Its principal purposes are to aid in the development of sound public policies and to promote public understanding of issues of national importance.

The Institution was founded December 8, 1927, to merge the activities of the Institute for Government Research, founded in 1916, the Institute of Economics, founded in 1922, and the Robert Brookings Graduate School of Economics and Government, founded in 1924.

The general administration of the Institution is the responsibility of a self-perpetuating Board of Trustees. The Trustees are likewise charged with maintaining the independence of the staff and fostering the most favorable conditions for creative research and education. The immediate direction of the policies, program, and staff of the Institution is vested in the President, assisted by the division directors and an advisory council, chosen from the professional staff of the Institution.

In publishing a study, the Institution presents it as a competent treatment of a subject worthy of public consideration. The interpretations and conclusions in such publications are those of the author or authors and do not purport to represent the views of the other staff members, officers, or trustees of the Brookings Institution.

Foreword

THE SUPREME COURT's decision in the case of *Baker v. Carr,* handed down in the spring of 1962, opened the way for reform of antiquated and inequitable patterns of representation in state legislatures. Over the ensuing twelve months, districting arrangements have been challenged in many states, and in several of them the legislatures have convened to draw up new districts which better reflect their actual population distribution.

The Court's decision has raised a number of issues, including the question whether the drive for more equal representation in the state legislatures will affect the United States Congress. The Brookings Institution therefore asked Professor Andrew Hacker, of the Department of Government, Cornell University, to prepare a problem paper that would examine the present congressional districts from the viewpoint of the problems that might arise in connection with reapportionment in the states. The objective was a brief informative analysis drawing largely on available materials, with an early deadline precluding much new research.

Mr. Hacker's report approaches this subject from several vantage points. Among these are: the constitutional and historical background of congressional districting; state and judicial action as it applies to the Congress; reasons for the disproportion between votes cast and seats won; and the extent and consequences of inequalities in representation in the House of Representatives. Mr. Hacker indicates that the House does not give an equal voice to all of its constituents, and that prevailing inequities may become even more pronounced since the forces opposing reform feel strongly that justice is on their side, and the courts have yet to indicate how far they will go in applying the doctrine of equal representation enunciated in *Baker v. Carr*—or, indeed, whether they will apply it at all to congressional districts.

The Institution and the author are grateful to those who read and commented on this study while it was in manuscript form. These included George A. Graham, Director of Governmental Studies, and Milton C. Cummings, Jr., Laurin L. Henry, M. Kent Jennings, F. P. Kilpatrick, and Harold Orlans of the Brookings staff; and also Stephen K. Bailey, Frank Munger, and Douglas Price of Syracuse University. Much of the preliminary statistical analysis was done by Mr. Hacker's students in his Seminar in Political Behavior at Cornell University; this work was checked and organized by Mrs. Jean Curtis of Ithaca, New York. Mrs. Virginia Parker edited the manuscript. Mrs. Helen Eisenhart prepared the index. Final thanks are owed to the indispensable *Congressional Quarterly* for providing population and voting figures for congressional districts.

The views expressed are those of the author and do not purport to represent the views of the trustees, officers, or other staff members of the Brookings Institution, or of the other readers of the manuscript.

ROBERT D. CALKINS
President

March 1963

Foreword to the Revised Edition

In 1964, the Supreme Court ruled in *Wesberry v. Sanders* and *Reynolds v. Sims* that congressional districts and the districts of both houses of bicameral state legislatures should be based on population. In this revision of his book Mr. Hacker has considered the effects of these decisions.

ROBERT D. CALKINS
President

September 1964
The Brookings Institution
1775 Massachusetts Avenue, N.W.
Washington, D.C.

Contents

Tables

1

Equal Votes for Equal Citizens?

EVERY TWO YEARS Americans enter polling places throughout the nation to vote for members of the United States House of Representatives. In theory, these voters are all equally participating citizens in the electoral system; in practice, their ballots are not of equal value.

One of the chief determinants of the value of a vote is the size of the district in which a citizen lives, for the eventual question is: with how many of his neighbors must a voter "share" his representative in the House? As an example, take the districting arrangements in Michigan during the 88th Congress, which was elected in November 1962 to serve until the end of 1964. According to the 1960 Census, the population of Michigan's 16th Congressional District was 802,994; that of the 12th District was 177,431. Thus, the constituents in the 16th District shared their congressman with four and a half times as many people as did those in the 12th. Put another way, those living in the 12th District had four and a half times as much representation in Washington, for all congressmen have an equal vote once they are sworn in as members of the House of Representatives. Put still another way, if the residents of the 16th District are regarded as having one vote apiece, their fellow citizens in the 12th District are each able to cast what amounts to four and a half votes.

Michigan is not a unique example. In Texas, the congressional district embracing the city of Dallas is over four times as populous as a rural district adjacent to it. In Colorado, the congressional district containing Boulder is more than three times the size of a district at the other end of the state. And in Ohio, the district with Dayton at its center is roughly three times as large as the congressional district in

1

which Zanesville is the largest city. These instances represent glaring disparities in voting power, but only slightly less disturbing disparities are very widespread. Of the 42 states with more than one congressional district after the 1960 Census, exactly half contain constituencies where the vote of a citizen in the smallest congressional district is worth at least twice that of the citizen in the largest district. These states, as well as those with more equitable representation, are shown in Table 1.

Inequities in legislative apportionment have recently been increasingly scrutinized in all parts of the country and at all levels of the political system. The initial impetus for this came from the first of three landmark Supreme Court decisions (all to be discussed in greater detail in later chapters). In *Baker v. Carr*, handed down in March 1962, the Court ruled that each citizen is guaranteed the "equal protection" of the laws required by the Fourteenth Amendment only if he can participate equally in selecting the members of his state legislature. The suit originated in Tennessee, where a ballot cast for a member of the Assembly's lower house by a citizen in a sparsely populated district was worth 23 times as much as one cast by a citizen in the most populated district. In February 1964 the Court invalidated Georgia's congressional districts, interpreting Article I, Section 2, of the Constitution as requiring that districts for the House of Representatives be substantially equal in population. This case, *Wesberry v. Sanders*, was initiated by citizens of Atlanta who protested that their share of a U.S. congressman was less than half that accorded to voters elsewhere in the state. And in June 1964, in *Reynolds v. Sims* and a series of related cases, the Court said that the districts of both houses of a bicameral state legislature could be apportioned by no standard other than population.[1]

In this chapter the precedents for equality of votes in the United States are discussed. Subsequent chapters will consider the judicial relationship to the problem of legislative redistricting; how and why states give added weight at the polls to some citizens and discriminate against others; and what future changes seem likely.

Throughout, for fairly obvious reasons, the focus will be on representation in the lower house of the United States Congress rather than in the Senate. Most Americans have been taught to accept the princi-

---

[1] *Baker v. Carr*, 82 S. Ct. 691; *Wesberry v. Sanders*, 84 S. Ct. 531; *Reynolds v. Sims*, 84 S. Ct. 1362.

TABLE 1. *Congressional Districts in 42 States: Value of Votes in Smallest District Compared to One Vote in Largest*[a]

State	Value Vote in Smallest District (Largest=1)	State	Value Vote in Smallest District (Largest=1)
Michigan	4.5	North Carolina	1.8
Texas	4.4	Utah	1.8
Arizona	3.3	Pennsylvania	1.8
Colorado	3.3	Virginia	1.7
Ohio	3.1	Kentucky	1.7
Maryland	2.9	Arkansas	1.7
Tennessee	2.8	Idaho	1.6
Florida	2.8	Montana	1.5
Georgia	2.8	Washington	1.5
South Dakota	2.7	Kansas	1.4
Illinois	2.5	West Virginia	1.4
Indiana	2.4	Iowa	1.3
Oklahoma	2.4	Massachusetts	1.3
New Jersey	2.3	Minnesota	1.3
Connecticut	2.2	Missouri	1.3
Wisconsin	2.2	Nebraska	1.3
Mississippi	2.1	New York	1.3
Louisiana	2.0	New Hampshire	1.2
California	2.0	Rhode Island	1.2
Oregon	2.0	Maine	1.1
South Carolina	2.0	North Dakota	1.1

[a] Source, *Congressional Redistricting: Impact of the 1960 Census Reapportionment of House Seats*, Special Report of Congressional Quarterly Service, September 28, 1962. Representatives in the 88th Congress, which opened in January 1963, were elected in November 1962 from districts based on the 1960 Census. In the eight states not included in this table, citizens enjoyed equal representation. Alaska, Delaware, Nevada, Vermont, and Wyoming have one congressman apiece; hence, each forms a single district. Hawaii and New Mexico have two congressmen each, both elected on an at-large basis. As a result of changes following the 1960 Census, all eight of Alabama's congressmen were elected at large in 1962; however, the intention is to divide the state into eight districts before the 1964 elections.

ple of a bicameral legislature, especially with respect to the structure of the national government. Youngsters learn that the states created the Union and that the Senate was created to symbolize the states' sovereign status. Everyone knows that New York and Alaska, California and Nevada, have two senators apiece, despite their overpowering differences in population. This basic constitutional arrangement apparently has the consent of even the citizens of the most populous states. Indeed, there is seldom an outcry about "minority rule" if the Senate passes or defeats a bill. (There is, of course, such an outcry when a Senate minority tries to keep legislation from coming to a vote.)

Recent attention, therefore, has been directed mainly to the United States House of Representatives. Is it or is it not a representative body? One rather compelling line of reasoning on this subject follows: If there are to be two legislative chambers, then at least one of them should represent all citizens of the nation on a basis of equality. The demand is for only half a loaf; minorities may be able to prevail in the Senate, but the majority should have its way in the House. According to this approach, the problem is that the House, too, is a distorted mirror of the population because congressional districts are of unequal size. If the lower chamber is to serve as a counterweight to the Senate, this argument proceeds, then it should at least accord an equal standing to all of its constituents. As the Senate is not bound by this principle, it is all the more incumbent on the House to give the principle precise expression.

Political Equality and the American Tradition

"The notion that representation proportioned to the geographic spread of population is . . . 'the basic principle of representative government' is, to put it bluntly, not true." Thus wrote Associate Justice Felix Frankfurter for the minority in his dissenting opinion to *Baker v. Carr*. And he continued: "However desirable and however desired among the great political thinkers and framers of our government, it has never been generally practiced, today or in the past. It was not the English system, it was not the colonial system, it was not the system chosen for the national government by the Constitution, it was not the system exclusively or even predominantly practiced by the States at the time of adoption of the Fourteenth Amendment, it is not predominantly practiced by the States today."[2]

Justice Frankfurter's minority opinion raised some interesting historical and philosophical questions concerning legislative representation in this country. It is no easy task to discover an "American tradition" on this subject, and the problem is complicated by the fact that conflicting "traditions" are often found by students who have in mind the

[2] *Baker v. Carr*, 82 S. Ct. 691, 756 (1962).

answers they are looking for. It certainly can be shown that the members of the colonial assemblies did not represent districts of equal size. "From the valley of the Susquehanna to that of the Savannah," Allan Nevins has written, "the settlers of the back country . . . were deprived of due political rights by unjust discrimination in the matter of representation."[3] Yet, when the colonies declared themselves states and proceeded to elect legislatures to draft their own constitutions, not a few rectified the imbalances that had existed prior to independence. The 89 members of New Hampshire's legislature were apportioned among that state's five counties in line with the distribution of population. In New York, similar standards of equity were observed. Under colonial rule, Pennsylvania had witnessed serious underrepresentation of the counties on its western frontier. But in allocating delegates to the 1776 convention to frame the state constitution, Philadelphia and the three eastern counties were given 24 members and the eight inland counties received twice that number, accurately reflecting the population spread. On the other hand, Virginia, Maryland, and South Carolina perpetuated old disparities. At the South Carolina constitutional convention, for example, counties with one-quarter of the population had 144 delegates whereas the remaining counties were allotted only 40.[4]

Certainly, unequal representation has a long history, and in this sense it is part of the American tradition. No less important, however, is the pattern of development over time. For a tradition has branches as well as roots, and its growth and direction are as significant as its origins. The fact that several states changed from unequal to equal representation at the time of independence may be more significant than the fact that others did not.

The Constitution: Framers and Ratifiers

Deducing the "intentions" of the framers of the Constitution is a time-honored vocation and avocation of judges, lawyers, and scholars. There are, generally speaking, four sources that may be drawn upon

[3] Allan Nevins, *The American States During and After the Revolution* (Macmillan, 1924), p. 114.
[4] *Ibid.*, pp. 132-33.

in an effort to discover the intended meaning of the Constitution. These are: (1) A close reading of the Constitution itself. (2) The recorded discussions and debates of the framers while at the Philadelphia convention. (3) *The Federalist*, the semiofficial interpretation of the document by Alexander Hamilton, John Jay, and James Madison. (4) The recorded deliberations of the state conventions that ratified the Constitution. It is worth exploring each of these sources to see what, if anything, was said about districting procedures for the House of Representatives.

The Constitution Itself

The Constitution itself does not state that congressional districts must be of equal or near-equal size. It does not require that a state create districts at all, but simply indicates that each state will be allotted a certain number of representatives. The relevant passages are in Section 2 of Article I.

> The House of Representatives shall be composed of Members chosen every second Year by the People of the several States, and the Electors in each State shall have the Qualifications requisite for Electors of the most numerous Branch of the State Legislature. . . .

> Representatives . . . shall be apportioned among the several States which may be included within this Union, according to their respective Numbers, which shall be determined by adding to the whole Number of free Persons, including those bound to Service for a Term of Years, and excluding Indians not taxed, three fifths of all other Persons. The actual Enumeration shall be made within three Years after the first Meeting of the Congress of the United States, and within every subsequent Term of ten Years, in such Manner as they shall by Law direct. The Number of Representatives shall not exceed one for every thirty Thousand, but each State shall have at Least one Representative; . . .

The first passage implies that the House of Representatives, in contrast to the Senate, will represent people rather than states. It follows that if the states are to have equal representation in the upper chamber then individuals are to be equally represented in the lower body. Phrased differently, if each state is to count for one in the Senate it follows that each citizen is to count for one in the composition of the House. The only way for this to be achieved is either for all of a state's representatives to be elected on an at-large basis or for the districts within each state to be of equal size.

The second passage provides that congressional apportionment among the states must be according to population. The Constitution nowhere says that each state, once in possession of its congressional delegation, must in turn create a separate district for each representative. Indeed, in the early years of the Republic, many states elected all of their representatives on at-large basis. This arrangement at least had the virtue of giving a vote of equal weight to all citizens, thus implementing the idea that the House of Representatives was to be based on population and no other considerations. There is little point in giving the states congressmen "according to their respective Numbers" if the states do not redistribute the members of their delegations on the same principle. For representatives are not the property of the states, as are the senators, but rather belong to the people who happen to reside within the boundaries of those states. Thus, each citizen has a claim to be regarded as a political unit equal in value to his neighbors.

To be sure, the Constitution allowed the individual states to decide who was to be able to vote in congressional elections. All those who could participate in electing "the most numerous Branch of the State Legislature" were eligible to cast ballots for representatives. Thus, if there were local property qualifications for state legislative elections, those qualifications would prevail for choosing congressmen. But this rule simply narrowed the electorate, or the number of "People" recognized as effective citizens. The presumption remains that all of these effective citizens, whether a small or large proportion of the total adult population of a state, should have votes of equal weight in electing representatives.

The Philadelphia Convention

The assemblage at the Philadelphia Convention was by no means committed to popular government, and few of the delegates had sympathy for the habits or institutions of democracy. Indeed, most of them interpreted democracy as mob rule and assumed that equality of representation would permit the spokesmen for the common man to outvote the beleaguered deputies of the uncommon man. "The evils we experience flow from the excess of democracy," Elbridge Gerry said. "The people do not want virtue, but are the dupes of pretended patriots."[5] Alexander Hamilton shared this view, asking a question to which he felt he already knew the answer: "Can a democratic assembly, who annually revolve in the mass of the people, be supposed steadily to pursue the public good?"[6] And Gouverneur Morris warned against "the dangerous influence of those multitudes without property and without principle, with which our country, like all others, will in time abound."[7]

But can these sentiments be taken to mean that the House of Representatives should be so arranged that Hamilton's "mass of the people" and Morris' "multitudes without property" would be given a smaller voice than sheer numbers would warrant? It is true that many participants at the Convention were unhappy about the existence of the House, let alone its composition. The framers made certain that the House would be counterbalanced by an aristocratic Senate, and that both branches of Congress could be checked by a president who was not popularly elected. Moreover, it was ensured, as has been pointed out, that the franchise for congressional elections could be limited by state voting laws.

At only one point in the Convention did the specific question of unequal legislative representation arise. Having in mind the composition of such legislatures as Maryland, South Carolina, and his own Virginia, Madison commented:

> The inequality of the representation in the legislatures of particular states would produce a like inequality in their representation in the national legislature, as it was presumable that the counties having the power in the former case would secure it to themselves in the latter.[8]

[5] In Max Farrand, *Records of the Federal Convention of 1787* (Yale University Press, 1937), Vol. I, p. 48.
[6] *Ibid.*, Vol. I, p. 299.
[7] *Ibid.*, Vol. II, p. 202.
[8] *Ibid.*, Vol. II, p. 241.

And the import of Madison's statement was that such unequal districting should be prevented. The occasion was his defense and explanation of Section 4 of Article I of the Constitution, which would give to the Congress the power to regulate "the times, places and manner of holding elections" for its own members. The chief use of that provision would be the national legislature's intervention if and when state legislatures failed to give equitable representation to their citizens. There is no recorded discussion on this point at the Philadelphia Convention—it subsequently arose at the state conventions—and apparently Madison's view was not contested even by his colleagues who had been so disparaging about the principles of political equality.

Why was it that Hamilton, Gerry, and Morris did not voice any criticism of a constitutional provision designed to ensure equal representation for all voters in House elections? Because the record is silent, it is necessary to speculate on what the conservative position was at that time. The question would have two sides to it. On the one hand, it is safe to assume that while the conservatives felt free to condemn the "mass" and the "multitudes," they were not against urban centers. It seems certain that the types of men they would have liked to see in the House of Representatives would come from such cities as New York, Boston, and Philadelphia. When it came to districting, they would have preferred that the cities receive at least a fair share of seats, simply because they would want as many places as possible for their own kind of people. To be sure, a necessary accompaniment of this view was that the franchise would be restricted to men of property, for otherwise the urban "multitudes" might elect a different kind of person to office. But given a limited urban electorate, Hamilton and his colleagues certainly would not have objected to intervention by Congress in order to ensure that the cities did not suffer discrimination.

The second side of the question would reflect a fear of the potential power of the inland farmers, most of whom did own property and consequently could not be denied the vote. The conservatives viewed the hinterland with mixed feelings; they certainly did not look on such areas as a bulwark against the excesses of popular democracy. In fact, the rural population was showing what conservatives would describe as dangerous signs of radicalism in many sections, or at least opposition to the growth of national power. Clearly, the conservatives were aware of what had happened in Pennsylvania in 1776, when the farmers of the western frontier had managed to gain a majority of seats in their state's legislature. The rural areas did, of course, have a majority of the population in all of the states. But in an exuberance of radical feeling, might they not use their power of numbers to weaken urban representation in the legislatures, and thus in the Congress? In sum, it may be suggested that Madison's call for equitable representation was regarded as a device to protect the urban minority against the rural majority. This is an understandable position if it is assumed that the urban electorates will be either restricted in size or deferential to the men of superior intellect and attainments in their midst. And this, no doubt, was the conservatives' hope.

The Federalist Papers

Once the Constitution was drafted and the Convention adjourned, various framers turned to the practical business of ratification. The best remembered product of this enterprise is *The Federalist*, the 85 essays supporting the Constitution written by Hamilton, Jay, and Madison, and addressed to the citizens of New York. The arguments of *The Federalist* were stated rather more prudently than those expressed behind the closed doors of the Convention sessions, for among the readers would be members of the "masses" and the "multitudes," who had to be persuaded that they would be represented under the proposed Constitution.

What *The Federalist* adds to the Convention proceedings is a more specific commentary on how the states were expected to distribute their congressional delegations. In Number 57, Madison stated that "each Representative of the United States will be elected by five or six thousand citizens."[9] This is revealing in several respects. First, it assumes that the states would create a district for each congressman rather than having them all elected at large. For five or six thousand would be the number of voters per constituency, not in the state as a

---

[9] Clinton Rossiter (ed.), *The Federalist Papers* (Mentor, 1961), p. 354.

whole. Second, it seems to presuppose that the districts would be fairly equal in size, ranging from about five to six thousand voters. If Madison thought that districts would have significantly unequal populations, he would not have suggested these figures. Third, it gives a fair estimate of the proportion of voters to the total population. According to the Constitution, every state could receive a representative for 30,000 of its inhabitants, with slaves counting as three-fifths of a person. It may be supposed that, given the life expectancies of the time, about half of the 30,000 residents of a district would be over the age of 21. Of these 15,000 adults, probably half were women who could not vote, leaving approximately 7,500 adult males. Thus, in suggesting that the electorate of each district would number between 5,000 and 6,000, Madison seemed to be forecasting that somewhere between two-thirds and three-quarters of the men over 21 would have the vote. (In districts with large proportions of slaves the percentages, of course, would be different.) If, in fact, this was what Madison meant, then his forecast ran counter to the theories favoring restricted electorates held by so many of his Convention colleagues. Needless to say, future developments substantiated the Madison figures rather than his colleagues' plea for a limited franchise.

At another point in Number 57, Madison gave a further indication that the states were intended to create several districts of equal size. After discussing the probable manner of congressional elections in New Hampshire and New York, he noted that "Pennsylvania is an additional example," and continued:

> Some of her counties, which elect her state representatives, are almost as large as her districts will be by which her Federal Representatives will be elected. The city of Philadelphia is supposed to contain between fifty and sixty thousand souls. It will therefore form nearly two districts for the choice of Federal Representatives.[10]

Thus, he supposed that a state like Pennsylvania would create districts for electing the various members of its House delegation and that each district would embrace about 30,000 people. It is interesting, also, that Madison thought Philadelphia would form two districts. Apparently he did not consider the possibility that districts might run from the

[10] *Ibid.*, p. 355.

city out into the countryside, thus combining urban and rural voters in a single constituency and thereby giving extra advantage to one or another interest.

The tenor of Madison's remarks in *The Federalist*, if they are taken as expressive to some degree of the framers' "intentions," is quite clear. The votes of citizens in congressional elections were to be given approximately equal weight insofar as this could be guaranteed by creating districts of equal size. Furthermore, if "the people" were to be represented in the House they were to be a substantial proportion of the adult male population and not simply a selective group defined by property and family connections.

The State Conventions

Since the states had to ratify the Constitution, the deliberations of the ratifiers presumably are part of the legislative history of that document. The discussions in the state conventions concerning the possibility of unequal congressional districts emphasized the power of the Congress to regulate in this area. In several states, it was questioned whether Congress should have jurisdiction over the "times, places and manner of holding elections." Patrick Henry, at the Virginia Convention, said that "the power over the manner admits of the most dangerous latitude."[11] And in Massachusetts, Samuel Nason said, "this is the article which is to make Congress omnipotent."[12] There were fears that an incumbent Congress might seek to perpetuate itself in power by overriding state election laws.

But it was also pointed out that unrepresentative state legislatures might abuse their districting powers, and that Congress should at least be able to ensure that each citizen of a state would have an equal vote when it came to selecting members of the House of Representatives. Interestingly, in this connection, South Carolina was held up as an example at more than one state convention. In Massachusetts, Rufus King said:

> The city of Charleston has a right to send thirty representatives to the General Assembly; the whole number of which amounts to two

[11] Jonathan Elliot (ed.), *The Debates of the Several State Conventions on the Adoption of the Federal Constitution* (Lippincott, 1876), Vol. 3, p. 175.
[12] *Ibid.*, Vol. 2, p. 136.

hundred. The back parts of Carolina have increased greatly since the adoption of their constitution, and have frequently attempted an alteration of this unequal mode of representation but the members from Charleston, having the balance so much in their favor, will not consent to an alteration; and we see that the delegates from Carolina in Congress have always been chosen by the delegates of that city. The representatives, therefore, from that state, will not be chosen by the people but will be the representatives of a faction of that state. If the general government cannot control in this case, how are the people secure?[13]

James Madison, speaking to the Virginia Convention, echoed his words:

> It was thought that the regulation of time, places and manner of electing the Representatives should be uniform throughout the continent. Some states might regulate the elections on the principles of equality, and others might regulate them otherwise. This diversity would be obviously unjust. Elections are regulated now unequally in some states, particularly South Carolina, with respect to Charleston, which is represented by thirty members. Should the people of any state by any means be deprived of the right of suffrage, it was judged proper that it should be remedied by the general government.[14]

And in South Carolina itself, Charles Cotesworth Pinckney, himself a resident of overrepresented Charleston, affirmed that it was "absolutely necessary that Congress should have this superintending power, lest, by the intrigues of a ruling faction in a state, the members of the House of Representatives should not really represent the people of the state."[15]

It cannot be argued that the views of King, Madison, and Pinckney—all of whom were at the Philadelphia Convention—were typical of the sentiments held by the hundreds of men who foregathered at the various state conventions. Nevertheless, it is clear that the opinion that unequal districts were evil and should be prevented or remedied was expressed during the ratification process. Men might differ on whether Congress should have the power to direct the "manner"

[13] *Ibid.*, Vol. 2, pp. 50-51.
[14] *Ibid.*, Vol. 3, p. 367.
[15] *Ibid.*, Vol. 4, p. 303.

in which the states conducted elections. But if fears were expressed over this power, it was because of more general anxieties, and not because of a feeling that congressional districts of unequal size ought to be defended.

There is, then, a good deal of evidence that those who framed and ratified the Constitution intended that the House of Representatives have as its constituency a public in which the votes of all citizens were of equal weight. In the final analysis, the aristocratic pronouncements of Hamilton, Gerry, and Morris cannot be regarded as having been written into the document's provisions dealing with the lower chamber of the national legislature. The House of Representatives was designed to be a popular chamber, giving the same electoral power to all who had the vote. And the concern of Madison, King, and Pinckney that districts be equal in size was an institutional step in the direction of securing this democratic principle.

The Democratic Impulse

In the half century following the drafting and ratification of the Constitution, the tendency towards thoroughgoing political equality was increasingly accentuated. James Kent, a spiritual heir of the Federalists, could lament:

> The progress and impulse of popular opinion is rapidly destroying every constitutional check, every conservative element intended by the sages who framed the earliest American constitutions, as safeguards against the abuses of popular suffrage.[16]

This was the age of Jackson, the equalitarian America that Alexis de Tocqueville saw and memorialized. Property qualifications for the vote disappeared and the people were using the ballot to reshape their institutions of government. The great catalyst was the adoption of new state constitutions during the 1830's.

These new constitutions were democratic documents in form as well as in substance. They were long, detailed, explicit. The assumption

[16] Quoted in Alfred de Grazia, *Public and Republic* (Knopf, 1951), p. 116.

was that even the elected officeholders were not to be trusted; consequently, their discretionary powers had to be held in check. The state constitutions served as popular referendums; they were ratified by the voters and subject to continual amendment by the same process. Elections for state officials and presidential electors were also by direct vote, the latter step being a serious modification of the framers' intentions. State legislators were held to short terms and a premium was placed on rotation in office. In the political parties, open nominating conventions were substituted for the closed caucuses in which candidates previously had been chosen. Members of the United States House of Representatives were not only elected directly by their constituents, but many states adopted the practice of instructing their congressmen on how to vote once they arrived at the Capitol.

The impact of the Jacksonian revolution was psychological as well as constitutional. Americans came to believe that they were all political equals, and they were prepared to act on that belief. The idea that one man, no matter what his origins or attainments, is as good as another became ingrained in the national character. This view may have been touched with arrogance—or naivete—but it is significant that the United States took the rhetoric of democracy seriously.

The democratic die was cast before the Civil War, and it only remained for the gradual removal of existing discriminations. The Fourteenth Amendment stated citizenship rights which could not be abridged, and the Fifteenth gave the vote to all male citizens regardless of race, color, or previous conditions of servitude.[17] The Fourteenth Amendment had a detailed provision on the question of representation, saying that if ballots were denied to a group of qualified voters in a state, then that state's delegation in the House of Representatives could be reduced in proportion to the number of disenfranchised citizens. While this provision has never been enforced, it makes clear that the Congress ought not to contain men purporting to represent constituents who have not been allowed to vote. The Seventeenth Amendment in 1913 took election of United States senators away from state legislatures and gave this power to the general electorate. And the Nineteenth Amendment, ratified in 1920, granted the

---

[17] Ratified in 1868 and 1870, respectively.

vote to women on an equal basis with men. The post-Civil War development of the Constitution on the rights of voters, then, has been on equalitarian premises that have been in evidence since the birth of the Republic. The enforcement of voting rights, it goes without saying, has often been a different matter. But here it need only be said that the registrar who refuses to register Negroes knows that he is acting in defiance of settled law, even if he persists for reasons that seem right to him.

Today, any American who is told that his vote has half the value of another man's will demand to know why, whether or not he ultimately decides that it is worth making a fuss about the inequity. The principle of "one man, one vote"—of an equal franchise for equal citizens—is part of the attitude that Americans cannot be divided on the grounds that one is somehow "superior" to another. There are no superiors and inferiors, at least in the political arena, and electoral arrangements that suggest this have the burden of proof placed on them.

Justice Frankfurter's reading of the American political tradition was, at best, a partial one. In citing instances of unequal representation in the past, and even the present, he missed the main line of development that has affected not only the Constitution but also the expectations of the American people. Advances were being made toward the goal of representation proportionate to population even before the decision in *Baker v. Carr*. Moreover, there are good reasons for believing that the framers of the Constitution intended that the Congress be chosen by voters with ballots of equal weight. But even if they had no such intention, the experience of subsequent decades has demonstrated that Americans work on the assumption that all citizens are equal and, therefore, entitled to votes of equal value.

2

The States and the Judiciary

THE PROBLEM OF REAPPORTIONING congressional districts is closely related to the composition of the state legislatures that create the congressional districts. For it is not likely that state legislatures that are themselves unrepresentative will care much about equality of representation in the constituencies they devise for United States congressmen. Considerable light is thrown on this relationship by two suits brought by Kenneth Colegrove of Illinois in the mid-1940's, as well as by the more recent *Baker v. Carr* case.

Colegrove's Cases

Kenneth Colegrove, a member of the Department of Political Science at Northwestern University, sued Governor Dwight Green of Illinois in 1946. Colegrove's complaint was that he was not being fairly represented in the Congress, and that this discrimination against him resulted from no other reason than the location of his home. He happened to live in what was then the 7th Congressional District of Illinois, a constituency with a population of 914,053. By way of contrast, the Fifth District contained only 112,116 people—all of whom had votes worth eight times as much as Colegrove's single ballot. It was suggested that this was an arbitrary discrimination giving added political advantage to some citizens by penalizing others.

The Supreme Court of the United States heard argument in *Colegrove v. Green* in early March 1946, and on June 10 handed down

17

its decision. By a vote of four to three, with two abstentions, the Court decided against Colegrove. In his opinion for the four-man majority, Associate Justice Felix Frankfurter stated that it was not for the judicial branch to decide questions so clearly "political" in character. He wrote:

> To sustain this action would cut very deep into the very being of Congress. Courts ought not to enter this political thicket. The remedy for unfairness in districting is to secure State legislatures that will apportion properly, or to invoke the ample powers of Congress.[1]

If inequities in representation exist, Justice Frankfurter suggested, there are two types of remedy available. On the one hand, the Congress itself has the power to regulate by law the "manner" in which its own members will be elected. Thus, it can require that all representatives come from districts of equal, or roughly equal, population. On the other hand, the state legislatures, which draw up congressional districts, can be pressured or persuaded to create constituencies of relatively equal size. But in either event, this responsibility was construed as being part of the legislative rather than the judicial process. Colegrove and others who felt underrepresented would have to work for the election of congressmen and state legislators sympathetic to the equalitarian principle. Their appeal must be to fellow citizens, and through them to the men who make national and state law. They must convince voters and legislators, not courts or judges, of the rightness of their cause. Justice Frankfurter concluded: "The Constitution has left the performance of many duties in our governmental scheme to depend . . . on the vigilance of the people in exercising their political rights."[2]

How helpful was this advice? It is true that the Congress has the power to legislate on the "manner" by which its members are chosen. Indeed, for nearly six decades, from 1872 to 1929, the apportionment acts had required that districts must contain "as nearly as practicable an equal number of inhabitants."[3] But this provision was not included

---

[1] *Colegrove v. Green*, 328 U. S. 549, 556 (1946).
[2] *Ibid.*
[3] 17 Stat. 28 (1872). The subsequent acts containing this provision were: 22 Stat. 5 (1882); 26 Stat. 735 (1891); 31 Stat. 733 (1901); and 37 Stat. 13 (1911).

in the 1929 act, nor in subsequent acts, and Congress had shown little inclination to revive it. Moreover, even when the requirement of equal-sized districts was on the books it was never enforced. During the entire 57 years, not a single representative was denied a seat because he had been elected by an undersized district, although there was obviously no shortage of candidates for such a challenge. Thus, to Colegrove, the chances of congressional action as a remedy undoubtedly appeared slender.

The alternative course was to elect state legislators who would be willing to draw up congressional districts in an equitable manner. But here Colegrove came upon another roadblock. He discovered that the districts for the Illinois legislature varied in size even more greatly than their congressional counterparts. One state senate district, for example, was 16 times as large as another. Moreover, Cook County, with 51 percent of the state's population, elected only 19 of the 51 state senators. In other words, a minority of the people of Illinois could fill 63 percent of the seats of the upper chamber. Thus, there would be little chance of electing a state legislature willing to create equal-sized congressional districts, even if Colegrove managed to persuade a majority of Illinois' voters to his way of thinking. There were, then, built-in obstacles to the democratic process that could not be surmounted by even the most vigorous exercise of democratic procedures.

Under these circumstances, Colegrove launched a second suit, this time against Edward J. Barrett, the Secretary of State of Illinois. He now asked the federal courts to order the Illinois legislature to redistrict itself along more equitable lines. It was obvious that the legislature would not do this unless compelled to do so, and a judicial directive seemed to be the only recourse. A three-man court of the Northern District of Illinois assumed jurisdiction in the case in December 1946, and the following February it handed down an adverse judgment. The case was then appealed directly to the Supreme Court of the United States. On March 10, 1947, that tribunal issued a brief statement refusing—six to three—to hear the case of *Colegrove v. Barrett*, explaining that the districting of state legislatures was outside its jurisdiction.[4]

---

[4] *Colegrove v. Barrett*, 330 U. S. 804 (1947). Associate Justices Hugo L. Black, William O. Douglas, and Frank Murphy were willing to hear the case.

The Supreme Court in its earlier opinion, written by Justice Frank-furter, had advised Colegrove to take his grievance directly to the peo-ple of his state. Yet, when Colegrove subsequently asked for judicial aid in establishing arrangements that would permit majority rule in Illinois, the Court—including Justice Frankfurter, despite his earlier opinion—refused to intervene. The Court seemed somewhat inconsist-ent in suggesting a program of action in one breath and, in the next, withholding the help needed to implement that course.

The State of the States

Even before the *Baker v. Carr* decision speeded action, extensive study was being given to questions of representation and misrepresen-tation as they were reflected in the 50 state legislatures. And there are good reasons for the increasingly close and sustained scrutiny of the states' districting arrangements. The postwar years witnessed fantastic changes in the face of American society, as movements of population that began during World War II accelerated. Tens of millions of Americans decamped from small towns and rural areas, moving to new jobs in urban centers. At the same time, there was a corresponding exodus from the large cities, seen in the outward migrations to the burgeoning suburbs. Although the countryside lost population and the suburbs gained, this was not a direct transfer. While one group of Americans was moving into the large and medium-sized cities, quite another type of group was moving out to the urban fringes.

The public soon began to notice that state legislatures were not responding to the new concentrations of population. Rural and small-town lawmakers continued to maintain majorities in the legislatures, and they displayed a marked indifference to the needs of both cities and suburbs. Urban and suburban citizens were cheerfully taxed, but their demands for legislation and appropriations were virtually ignored. Typical of the complaints was one voiced in 1959 before a congres-sional subcommittee studying apportionment:

Urban and suburban underrepresentation is one of the most notori-ous and shameful facts in American political life today. . . . Because of urban representation—because a city vote is worth only a fraction of what a country vote is worth—the severe, pressing problems of urban and suburban America are being neglected. . . . America is, today, an urban nation. A majority of the people of the Nation live in urban centers and their immediate environs. . . .[5]

Since virtually all state legislatures failed to reflect population distributions in their districting arrangements, they were a choice target. A classification by Paul T. David and Ralph Eisenberg of the nation's 3,000-odd counties into four population groups shows how patterns of residence have changed over a 50-year period.[6] As Table 2 shows, in 1910, 65.1 percent of all Americans lived in the 2,945 counties with

TABLE 2. *Number and Population of Counties in the United States, 1910 and 1960*[a]

Population of County	Counties		Population	
	Number	*Percentage*	Number (In thousands)	*Percentage*
IN 1910:				
Under 25,000	2,149	*70.5*	27,421	*29.9*
25,000–99,999	796	*26.1*	32,203	*35.2*
100,000–499,999	87	*2.9*	17,154	*18.7*
500,000 and over	15	*0.5*	14,853	*16.2*
Total	3,047	*100.0*	91,632	*100.0*
IN 1960:				
Under 25,000	1,942	*62.1*	23,064	*12.9*
25,000–99,999	884	*28.2*	41,247	*23.1*
100,000–499,999	238	*7.6*	48,542	*27.1*
500,000 and over	64	*2.1*	65,705	*36.9*
Total	3,128	*100.0*	178,558	*100.0*

[a] Source, Paul T. David and Ralph Eisenberg, *Devaluation of the Urban and Suburban Vote* (Bureau of Public Administration, University of Virginia, 1961), p. 8.

[5] Statement by Andrew J. Biemiller, lobbyist for the AFL-CIO, in *Standards for Congressional Districts (Apportionment)*, Hearings before Subcommittee No. 2 of the House Committee on the Judiciary, 86th Cong. 1st sess. (1959), p. 65.

[6] Paul T. David and Ralph Eisenberg, *Devaluation of the Urban and Suburban Vote* (Bureau of Public Administration, University of Virginia, 1961).

less than 100,000 residents. A half-century later, in 1960, only 36 percent of the country could be found in the 2,826 counties of less than
100,000. It is also significant that the number of sparsely settled counties did not decrease markedly during the 50-year period. Whereas in
1910, 96.6 percent of the counties had under 100,000 people in them,
the figure had fallen to only 90.3 percent by 1960. This, of course, was
because most of the nation's growth took place in a few concentrated
areas. The fact that so many small counties remain becomes important
when it is recalled that the county, regardless of population, has
tended to be the basic unit of state legislative representation.

Redistricting: Action and Inaction

State legislatures seem to have taken little or no notice of patterns
of movement within their borders. A National Municipal League report compiled midway through 1961 showed that 14 states had let at
least a decade elapse during which they had not redistricted their
lower chambers, and four states had lower houses based on districts
created prior to 1900.[7]

But too much emphasis can be given to when a state last engaged
in redistricting. The act of redrawing constituency boundaries need
not be a thoroughgoing enterprise, but rather a series of token adjustments. Moreover, redistricting is not necessarily guided by considerations of changing population distribution within the state. Seventeen
states redistricted their lower houses in the first half of 1961. To be
sure, since they acted before the Supreme Court decision on *Baker v.
Carr*, they had no overriding compunction to redistrict according to
the equal-population standard. Thus, it is interesting to see in Table 3
that quite substantial variations in size, hence the value of citizens'
votes, were written into most of the states' 1961 laws. Idaho, Iowa,
Missouri, Montana, Nevada, North Carolina, Ohio, and Oklahoma—
all of which redistricted in 1961—had higher ratios separating the
value of votes in their largest and smallest districts than did Indiana,
Kentucky, Massachusetts, Nebraska, and Wyoming, which had not

---

[7] William J. D. Boyd (ed.), *Compendium on Legislative Apportionment* (National Municipal League, 1962). Some of these states were redistricted in 1962 as a
result of *Baker v. Carr*, and others will take action in 1963.

acted since 1947, and the ratios were even higher than that in Maryland, which had not acted since 1867. What emerges is that the date of the last redistricting is less crucial than the rules guiding a legislature when it draws district lines.

TABLE 3. *Lower Houses of State Legislatures: Year of Last Redistricting Before Baker v. Carr and Value of Vote in Smallest District Compared to One Vote in Largest*[a]

Year of Last Redistricting	Value of Vote in Smallest District (Largest = 1)	Year of Last Redistricting	Value of Vote in Smallest District (Largest = 1)
PRIOR TO 1900:		1951–60 (*Continued*)	
New Hampshire	1,081.3	Colorado	8.1
Vermont	987.0	Virginia	7.1
Delaware	35.4	Alaska	6.4
Maryland	12.5	Arizona	5.3
		Washington	4.6
PERIOD 1901–50:		Michigan	4.0
Connecticut	424.5	Wisconsin	3.9
Rhode Island	39.0	Illinois	3.6
Tennessee	23.0	Hawaii	2.2
Mississippi	16.7		
Alabama	15.6	1961:	
Massachusetts	13.9	Nevada	31.4
Kentucky	6.0	Idaho	25.5
Indiana	5.4	Missouri	22.2
Wyoming	3.4	North Carolina	19.0
Nebraska	2.7	Iowa	17.8
		Ohio	14.5
PERIOD 1951–60:		Oklahoma	14.0
Florida	108.7	Montana	14.0
Georgia	98.8	North Dakota	7.5
Kansas	33.2	Texas	6.7
Pennsylvania	31.1	Maine	6.6
Utah	27.8	Arkansas	6.4
Louisiana	17.4	California	6.2
New Mexico	15.5	South Dakota	4.7
New York	14.8	New Jersey	4.6
Minnesota	13.3	South Carolina	3.1
West Virginia	9.0	Oregon	3.0

[a] Sources, David and Eisenberg, *Devaluation of the Urban and Suburban Vote, op. cit.*, p. 3; and William J. D. Boyd (ed.), *Compendium on Legislative Apportionment* (National Municipal League, 1962).

The most common of these rules, usually written into a state's constitution, is that every county in the state must have at least one representative in one or both of the legislative chambers. This representation of the counties, like that of states in the United States Senate, disregards the element of population. While populous counties are usually accorded several seats, they can be outvoted by the numerous smaller counties—all of which have a minimum of one spokesman. Thus, each of Iowa's 99 counties has a representative in the lower house, and each of the nine largest counties has a second seat. Fifty-eight of Iowa's counties in 1960 had a population of less than 20,000. Yet the 58 members representing 834,750 Iowans in these counties carried over three times as much weight in the lower house as 18 members from the nine largest counties, even though the latter represented 1,024,485 people.[8]

Rural Votes Compared to Urban Votes

The consequence of perpetuating outworn district lines, and of permitting counties as units to have equal or near-equal representation, has been to penalize citizens living in sections of the state that have been growing in population. As seen in Table 2, the number of counties in the country with populations of over 100,000 had grown from 102 in 1910 to 302 in 1960. It is the residents of these counties who have seen their votes devalued during the last half-century. David and Eisenberg computed the relative values of the votes of residents of four groups of counties in 1910 and 1960, covering the balloting for both houses of the state legislature. The norm they used for the value of one vote was the average value of a vote on a statewide basis. County variations from their state averages were then computed for groups of counties, classed by population, across the country. The results of this computation are given in the tabulation opposite.

Even in 1910, the residents of counties with a population of over 500,000 had four-fifths of a vote in contrast with their fellow citizens in counties of under 25,000, who had 1.13 votes. The ratio of electoral power between these two groups of Americans, therefore, was 1 to

[8] There is another curious feature in the Iowa system. The ninth largest county, with a population of 55,060, receives twice as many representatives as the tenth largest, with 49,894.

1.39. But, by 1960, while those residing in heavily populated counties saw their ballot fall in value to three-quarters of a vote, citizens who had remained in sparsely settled counties saw theirs rise to a value of 1.71 votes. Transposed in terms of a ratio, the relation between an urban and a rural vote was 1 to 2.25.[9] Put yet another way, in 1910, a city ballot was worth 72 percent of one cast in the countryside; in 1960 it was worth only 44 percent. (In the tabulation below, 1 equals the average statewide value of the vote.)

Value of Vote for State Legislature by Size of County, 1910 and 1960

Population of County	Value of Vote	
	1910	1960
Under 25,000	1.13	1.71
25,000-99,999	1.03	1.23
100,000-499,999	.91	.81
500,000 and over	.81	.76

The importance of the David-Eisenberg figures is that they indicate the value of the vote in all parts of the country, and not simply for selected districts. The contrast between the voting power of residents of the largest and smallest districts in a state may show some graphic discrepancies simply because it focuses on the most egregious inequities. Yet, if the country is taken as a whole it can be said that the average rural vote is worth something over twice the average urban vote, but not much more. To be sure, there are millions of Americans living in oversized legislative districts who can legitimately complain that their electoral influence is many times less than that of some other voters in their state. But it should be kept in mind that

[9] In these terms, the tabulation would read:

Population of County	Value of Vote	
	1910	1960
Under 25,000	1.39	2.25
25,000-99,999	1.27	1.62
100,000-499,999	1.12	1.07
500,000 and over	1.00	1.00

while comparisons of most-favored and least-favored citizens make vivid reading, such comparisons can also deflect attention from the overall picture.

Baker v. Carr

By the early 1960's, city dwellers knew, without elaborate statistical analysis, that their voice in the state legislatures was becoming increasingly muted. The advice handed down in *Colegrove v. Green*—"to secure state legislatures that will apportion properly"—was easy to give but hard to follow. In state after state, a majority of the voters had been sending their quota of lawmakers to the capitol only to discover that the majority of the legislature was elected by a minority of the voters. For example, in California, 11 percent of the voters could elect 51 percent of the state senate; in Florida, 12 percent could elect the majority. In Kansas, 19 percent of the electorate could select more than half the state's lower house; in Vermont, it took only 12 percent of the voters to choose the majority.

Tennessee, as these figures show, was by no means the worst off of the 50 states in terms of minority domination. With 27 percent of the voters being able to elect the majority of the upper house and 29 percent capable of electing the lower chamber, Tennessee fell about midway among the states.[10] Yet a group of Nashville citizens felt sufficiently aggrieved to take their case to the courts. They had tried the path laid down in *Colegrove v. Green* and it came to a deadend. Furthermore, they and others sensed—correctly—that the judiciary of 1962 might be more sympathetic to the problem of urban underrepresentation than the courts in 1946.

The Majority Opinion

On March 26, 1962, by a vote of six to two, the Supreme Court decided that legislative apportionment was a legitimate judicial issue. It might or might not be "political," but it was a responsibility the courts should be prepared to oversee. Speaking for the majority, As-

[10] Boyd, *Compendium on Legislative Apportionment, op. cit.,* pp. iii-iv.

sociate Justice William J. Brennan, Jr. pointed out that citizens who
are underrepresented have a "personal stake," and thus are entitled
to sue for relief. The issue of apportionment may affect every resident
of the state, but prevailing arrangements can create such disadvan-
tages for an individual city-dweller that he has a right to ask for general reform of legislative districting. But the Tennessee appellants had
a more specific complaint. The state's constitution and a 1901 act of
the legislature called for reapportionment every 10 years. Yet both
constitution and statute had been ignored for six decades, and representation in 1961 stood where it had been at the turn of the century.
Justice Brennan wrote:

> These appellants seek relief in order to protect or vindicate an
> interest of their own, and of those similarly situated. Their con-
> stitutional claim is, in substance, that the 1901 statute constitutes
> arbitrary and capricious state action, offensive to the Fourteenth
> Amendment in its irrational disregard of the standard of apportion-
> ment prescribed by the State's Constitution or of any standard,
> effecting a gross disproportion of representation to voting popula-
> tion. The injury which appellants assert is that this classification
> disfavors the voters in the counties in which they reside, placing
> them in a position of constitutionally unjustifiable inequality vis-a-vis
> voters in irrationally favored counties.[11]

The Supreme Court based its decision on the "equal protection of
the laws" clause of the Fourteenth Amendment. Citizens of Tennessee
who were underrepresented in the legislature could not have such
equal protection because they did not have equal participation in the
selection of the lawmakers. The Court, however, did not go so far as
to say how equal participation had to be. Notably, the justices did not
assert that all districts for both legislative chambers had to be based
on constituencies of equal or near-equal populations. Rather, as in the
school desegregation cases, this job was handed over to the lower
courts. Judges at the district level would decide whether existing or
proposed apportionment systems were equitable under the general
strictures of the Fourteenth Amendment. "We have no cause at this
stage to doubt the District Court will be able to fashion relief," Justice
Brennan said.[12]

[11] *Baker v. Carr*, 82 S. Ct. 691, 704-05 (1962).
[12] *Ibid.*, p. 699.

In a concurring opinion, Justice Douglas summarized the key point at issue: "The question is the extent to which a State may weight one person's vote more heavily than it does another's."[13] In another concurrence, Associate Justice Tom C. Clark answered that question by showing the disparate weightings assigned to votes cast in each of the state's counties. "The apportionment picture in Tennessee is a topsy-turvical of gigantic proportions," he wrote. "Tennessee's apportionment is a crazy quilt without rational basis."[14] While Justice Clark did not believe that precise numerical equality was demanded, the inequalities he had seen were more than reason could allow. In addition, he underlined the propriety of judicial intervention in this area. An earlier case had said that citizens had the "practical" option of voting in legislators mandated to redress the apportionment balance. This rule neglected to note that in many states the majority was, try as it might, unable to rule. Justice Clark said:

> The majority of the people of Tennessee have no "practical opportunities for exerting their political weight at the polls" to correct the existing "invidious discrimination." Tennessee has no initiative and referendum. I have searched diligently for other "practical opportunities" present under the law. I find none other than through the federal courts.[15]

Thus, the courts entered the "political thicket" against which Justice Frankfurter warned in *Colegrove v. Green*. And Justice Frankfurter remained steady in this view, although in 1962 he wrote as a dissenter rather than as spokesman for the Court majority.

Dissent by Justices Frankfurter and Harlan

The majority in *Baker v. Carr* had suggested that equal votes for equal citizens was a goal that might properly be pursued by judicial means. Associate Justices Frankfurter and John Marshall Harlan disagreed on both counts. Indeed, they raised the fundamental question as to whether equal representation in the lawmaking process was a valid principle. To their minds, majority rule was not a settled matter

[13] *Ibid.*, p. 723.
[14] *Ibid.*, p. 730.
[15] *Ibid.*, p. 732.

but still an issue of controversy; minorities might, in some circumstances, be entitled to disproportionate representation. At all events, whether or not minorities were so entitled, the dissenters felt the issues could not be decided by bland recourse to generalities. Justice Frankfurter said:

> One cannot speak of "debasement" or "dilution" of the value of a vote until there is first defined a standard of reference as to what a vote should be worth. What is actually asked of the Court in this case is to choose among competing bases of representation—ultimately, really, among competing theories of political philosophy.[16]

Justice Frankfurter, quite candidly, preferred one philosophy over another. He regarded the equalitarian theory as based more on emotion than either reason or practicality. His reading of the historical record did not persuade him that numerical equality was an unquestioned tenet of American government.

Those pressing for pure majority rule, he went on, were apparently unaware that minority rights have played a vital role in American institutions. Only a small minority of the states apportion both their houses by the population standard alone, with the majority of legislatures demonstrating that the democratic tradition does not have universal support. As noted in Chapter 1, Justice Frankfurter forthrightly denied the universal acceptance or practice of the theory that representation "proportioned to the geographic spread of population" is a standard of political equality.[17]

The tenor of his statement is that the status quo embodies both the historical and philosophical components of the American tradition. If majority rule is not "generally practiced" in selecting the memberships of state legislatures, then this suggests that minority rule should prevail in the future because it has prevailed in the past. On the other hand, if this history and philosophy are to be abrogated, then the equalitarian claim should be viewed as a proposal for reform. And the burden of justification lies with those who would jettison old arrangements in favor of some new, untried scheme.

Finally, Justice Frankfurter denied that the Supreme Court had any business intervening in the area. Proponents of wider democracy,

[16] Ibid., p. 755.
[17] Ibid., p. 756.

he felt, were asking the judiciary, an undemocratic institution, to make the decision rather than leaving it to the public at large:

> In this situation, as in others of like nature, appeal for relief does not belong here. Appeal must be to an informed, civically militant electorate. In a democratic society like ours, relief must come through an aroused popular conscience that sears the conscience of the people's representatives.[18]

The Justice presumably knew that between 27 percent and 29 percent of the Tennessee electorate could select the representatives who would constitute a majority of the legislature. If this majority were opposed to equitable apportionment, as it undeniably was, then a "militant electorate" would have to recruit as many as 71 percent of the voters before it could elect a legislature sympathetic to equal representation. In other words, in Tennessee it was necessary for a popular majority to receive almost three-quarters of the votes before it elected a majority of the legislators. Perhaps Justice Frankfurter felt that such an extraordinary majority was necessary to upset tradition and alter the existing pattern of representation. At all events, he would have allowed the status quo to persist until the "popular conscience" had become close to unanimous in favoring change. However, simple majority rule was operative in the Supreme Court itself, and Baker's case against Carr became law of the land.

Rhetoric and Reality

Justice Frankfurter was not alone in wondering whether his colleagues subscribing to the majority opinion in *Baker v. Carr* were not indulging in "merely empty rhetoric, sounding a word of promise to the ear, sure to be disappointing to the hope."[19] He may have had in mind the school desegregation decisions, handed down almost a decade earlier, which had been met with little more than token compliance in most parts of the country. To be sure, legislative apportionment did not appear to be the sort of issue that usually arouses popular emotions. On the whole it was a problem of direct concern to the politicians rather

[18] *Ibid.*, p. 739.
[19] *Ibid.*

than to the man-in-the-street.[20] At the same time Frankfurter and many others were becoming anxious over the impact of a whole series of recent Supreme Court cases on public sensibilities. Added together, the various decisions dealing with obscenity, school prayers, and criminal due process were creating the widespread impression that the federal judiciary was intervening in areas that rightfully belonged to the states and local communities. All that was needed was one more example of presumed judicial usurpation to ignite a veritable tinder box of resentment. While Frankfurter sounded this warning in many of his dissenting opinions, his admonition in *Baker v. Carr* is most likely to be remembered.

The Meaning of Equity

"No one," Justice Clark said in his *Baker v. Carr* concurrence, "contends that mathematical equality among voters is required by the equal protection clause."[21] And the Supreme Court was clear in pointing out that it was not ready to lay down standards of equitable representation. That was to be left to judges at lower levels, and it must be said that they have been drawing up practical criteria of their own. What this amounts to is that a particular judge will look at a reapportionment plan drawn up by a legislature and will then state whether he thinks it is "fair enough." This is obviously a rule of thumb (or a rule of reason) and depends on the tastes and sensibilities of the judges in question. However, a body of precedents is rapidly accumulating and even now courts are referring to actions taken elsewhere. Since some of these conflict with each other, the Supreme Court undoubtedly will have to make several new decisions before long.

The question of what is equitable representation is best summarized by considering the status of the second chamber of the state legislatures. The belief seems to be growing that at least one chamber will

---

[20] This was the general position taken in the first edition of this study. What was overlooked was the fact that if politicians become sufficiently concerned over a threat to their own interests they will try to arouse public sentiment on their side. Thus, in the Fall of 1964, legislative apportionment became an issue in both the Presidential campaign and on Capitol Hill. In an important sense this debate symbolized the clash between the "Two Americas," to be discussed in Chapter 5.

[21] *Baker v. Carr*, p. 732.

have to be apportioned on the sole basis of population, with each representative coming from districts of nearly equal size. By 1964, indeed in time for the primaries preceding the 1964 election, a majority of states in all likelihood will have completed cases requiring the redistricting of one house on a numerical basis. But 49 of the 50 states have a second chamber.[22] What rules govern its composition?

Most often heard is the argument that each state is a miniature "federal" system. Under this analogy, one chamber of the legislature may represent population but the other should represent other units. These may be counties or towns or simply land area,[23] but usually it is the county. In a few states each county has no more than one seat; for example, Los Angeles County has a single spokesman in the California senate. But in most states, every county has at least one seat, with more populous counties getting extra seats. Almost all states have at least one county with population of less than 5,000, represented by a state senator with a voice and a vote equal to that of all his colleagues. The "federal" view asserts that what usually amounts to county representation is legitimate for one chamber of the legislature. What is good for the United States Congress, it is reasoned, is good for the states. Judge O. Bowie Duckett of the Circuit Court of Anne Arundel County in Maryland inventoried the arguments for applying units of representation other than population to the state senate:

> Such an arrangement protects the minorities. It prevents hasty, although popular, legislation at the time. It is based upon history and reason and helps to protect the republican form of government guaranteed by . . . the United States Constitution. It preserves the checks and balances of the state governments which has worked so well under the federal. Moreover, there would be little advantage in having a bicameral legislature if the composition and qualifications of the members were similar.[24]

[22] Nebraska has a unicameral, or one-house legislature.

[23] The recently adopted Michigan constitution gives each of the 79 counties an "apportionment factor" determining how many state senators the county is to have. Eighty percent of the "factor" is based on population and 20 percent on the number of square miles in the county. Quite clearly it is not "land" that is being represented here; rather the sorts of people who live in sparsely settled areas are intended to be overrepresented. See William J. D. Boyd, *Patterns of Apportionment* (National Municipal League, 1962), pp. 17-18.

[24] Quoted in Robert B. McKay, *Reapportionment and the Federal Analogy* (National Municipal League, 1962), p. 4.

Each of these arguments can be questioned.

First: "Such an arrangement protects the minorities." This is so in the sense that it gives the residents of small towns and rural areas the legislative power to veto bills that displease them. It also gives these minorities the opportunity to deny larger cities and suburban areas the resources needed to solve their own problems. It is one thing to protect yourself from oppression; it is quite another to harass other sections of the community because you think they are inferior or undeserving types of people. Moreover, only selected minorities—certain minorities in the less populous areas—are protected. Negroes are not sheltered, nor are white citizens who experience discrimination due to their national origin or family background. Minorities espousing unconventional views are hardly protected; and an important minority group, the residents of suburbs—often unrecognized as a minority—are continually penalized because of underrepresentation. The question, very simply, is: Which minorities are allowed to safeguard their interests? The answer: Of all the minority groups that make up a state only a very few are given this advantage.

Second: "It prevents hasty, although popular, legislation. . . ." This has always been a persuasive argument. The theory—and it is only a theory—is that a lower chamber elected on the basis of population immediately translates mass sentiment into tyrannical or spendthrift legislation. The aristocratic second chamber then draws in the reins, wisely ponders the basic problem, and produces a rational solution by amending or rejecting the bill the lower house passed in haste. The trouble with this theory is that it has no basis in fact. For one thing, hasty legislation is difficult for either chamber because control of the agenda is usually in the hands of an entrenched group of party leaders or committee chairmen. State legislatures are not very susceptible to public opinion, temperate or intemperate. But when such legislatures do reflect mass emotions, as has happened when lawmakers in the Deep South have rushed through new segregation barriers, then both upper and lower chambers usually exhibit this failing. At all events, it is difficult to enumerate instances of oppressive bills that sailed through lower state houses and were then stopped by the upper house. And for such examples, matching cases can be shown where the lower house killed an excessive bill emanating from the upper chamber. One final rebuttal on this argument: Nebraska has had a unicameral legislature since the thirties, and its laws have been no more unreasoned than those of the other 49 states.

Third: "It is based upon history and reason and helps to protect the republican form of government. . . ." The national government has a bicameral Congress, with a Senate based on state representation, because this arrangement was necessary in order to establish the United States as a nation. Among the 13 states, the smaller ones would only agree to give up part of their sovereignty and join the Union if their interests were protected in a Senate where they would have an equal vote. There is nothing "reasonable" about the basis of representation of the Senate. What was reasonable was the action of the framers in settling for a compromise that would induce all the states to throw in their lot with the new venture. Moreover, the states created the Union and, hence, could demand representation, as states, as the price of giving up some of their identity. Counties are not sovereign. They are created by states and can be abolished by them, as some have. Few counties have historic identities, and all are administrative devices for performing certain functions at the local level. Certainly, the counties cannot claim to have created the states, as the states did the Union. Finally, the Fourteenth Amendment—requiring the states to grant equal protection to all their citizens—was adopted in 1868 and is evidence that the Constitution gives latest priority to personal equality. Representation of states in the Senate is a fact of history. But the general idea underlying it has neither been revived nor renewed.

Fourth: "It preserves the checks and balances of the state government which has worked so well under the federal." Checks and balances refer to the mutual controls that the executive, legislative, and judicial branches have over each other. It is a somewhat new construction to assert that two houses of a legislature are also intended to check and balance one another. If this is so then the result will probably be stalemate and ultimate inaction. And the consequence will be that power will gravitate away from both houses of the legislature, either to administrative agencies in the state or to the bureaus of the federal government. This is hardly the outcome that proponents of limited government want. On the contrary, their objectives could better be achieved by greater coordination between the two houses of the state legislature. Only in that way will the real threats be held in check.

Fifth: ". . . there would be little advantage in having a bicameral legislature if the composition and qualifications of the members were similar." In this instance, those who find all virtue in the status quo are unable to think seriously of workable alternatives.[25] Each citizen can be represented in more than one way, and each method may reflect his interests in a valid manner. Thus, part of his personality may be "local" and another part may be "national." Moreover, he may be one kind of person in 1958 and another kind in 1960. There is no reason why both chambers cannot be based on population, with districts of equal size for all senators. However, the lower house might have districts of 40,000, and each upper house might have a district of 160,000 covering four of the lower-chamber districts. In this way, a voter would have a "local" representative in the lower house and a spokesman with a "broader" view in the upper chamber. Furthermore, one house might be elected in 1961 and the other in 1963 so that the new thinking of the electorate would be reflected in one chamber at any given time. Or one could have two-year terms and the other six-year terms, thus sheltering one chamber from the necessity of worrying about reelection at frequent intervals. The point, of course, is that bicameralism can easily be based on an identical voting public. For that public can be represented in more than one way. Yet, no matter how deeply a voter's personality may be split or how much his moods vary over time, he is still a first-class citizen and is entitled to equal participation in electing the men who make his laws.

A Civil Rights Question

Any alternative to the population basis is bound to deny some citizen the equality posited by the Fourteenth Amendment. This was put well by William L. Taylor, who asked:

[25] See Boyd, *Patterns of Apportionment, op. cit.,* for at least nine different possibilities for constituting a second chamber, pp. 11-18.

When state action makes the vote of one citizen worth one quarter of the vote of another, how does the "character of the wrong" suffered differ from the case where the vote is denied a Negro on racial grounds? If a right to an undiluted vote exists, should not both actions be deemed a denial of equal protection of the laws?[26]

In short, the problem of inequitable representation will persist even if one chamber is reformed so as to be based solely on population. A city dweller may have his one vote for the lower house, but only half a vote for the upper chamber. His fellow citizen in a rural area will also have one vote for the state house of representatives but one and a half votes for the state senate. Thus, if the two elections are taken together, the urban resident has one and a half votes and his country cousin has two and a half—or 60 percent more influence in the electoral scales.

The analogy between Negroes who suffer discrimination and voters who are underrepresented has been a theme of this discussion. Both have been denied their civil rights as citizens, both have been deprived of equal status in society. Civil rights—unlike civil liberties—refer to the equality sought by entire groups of citizens.[27] That is, a person whose civil rights are abridged suffers penalties not because of what he has done as an individual (that would be a civil liberties question), but because of what he is in his role as a member of a group in society. Thus, a Negro is denied admission to first-class citizenship because he is a Negro, not because he has done anything in particular. Similarly, a citizen will have a diluted vote just because he happens to live in one section of the state, not because he as an individual has engaged in certain acts. Thus, the Negro and the city dweller cannot be held personally responsible for the disability they suffer. To be sure, the city dweller can move to the country just as the southern Negro can move to the North. But under the Constitution, one should not have to move one's family to a place where rights are guaranteed—they should be equally guaranteed everywhere.

---

[26] Quoted in editorial in *New Republic,* January 29, 1962, p. 5.

[27] For an elaboration of this difference, see Andrew Hacker, "The Indifferent Majority," *The New Leader,* March 18, 1963, pp. 18-21.

Applying the Principles

Along with its substantive impact on the distribution of legislative power within the states, *Baker v. Carr* will be remembered for the sheer volume of litigation it poured into the nation's courts. Within 20 months of the original decision, citizens in 39 of the 50 states had brought suits challenging prevailing districting arrangements. Moreover, in this same period no less than 20 states actually changed their apportionment schemes, more often than not because of an impending judicial order or the threat of one. The willingness of judges, on both federal and state levels, to implement *Baker v. Carr* was in itself noteworthy. "Lower courts did not wait for guidance from above," Anthony Lewis wrote in a *New York Times* summary. "They moved ahead in the expansion of a new constitutional doctrine with a speed for which legal observers can find no recent parallel."[28]

Yet the fact that 20 of the 50 states had embarked on redrawing their legislative maps could not in itself be taken as the end of the tale. In state after state, the courts examined the newly submitted districting patterns and—in most cases—found them sorely inadequate. In Tennessee, the birthplace of *Baker v. Carr,* plans were sent back and forth from capitol to courthouse three or more times, and at each juncture the judges announced that the latest revision was still unsatisfactory. "The rural bloc has demonstrated that it will seek every means of avoiding compliance—even cheating by a few seats—in an effort to preserve as much of its authority as possible," a correspondent in Nashville reported.[29] As a final resort Tennessee issued a call for a constitutional convention to draw up an apportionment scheme. But even here the question would arise as to the manner in which the delegates to such a convention were chosen; clearly one ground for challenging an apportionment plan would be to say that legislative districts created by an unrepresentative convention were themselves invalid. All in all, the states that redistricted during 1963 and 1964 only went through the motions of reform, with the result that appeals against these new plans began to follow *Baker v. Carr* up the well-trod road to the United States Supreme Court.

[28] *New York Times,* November 10, 1963.
[29] *Ibid.*

In only one state (Illinois) did the courts go so far as to require that legislative elections in 1964 be held on a statewide at-large basis, because an adequate redistricting plan had not been presented. An at-large balloting for members of a state legislature staggers the imagination, considering the degree to which local personalities and interests normally pervade such elections. The Illinois House of Representatives has a membership of 177; if both parties were allowed to file slates with 177 candidates the odds would be that most voters would be so confused by the array of unfamiliar names that they would simply cast a blanket vote on a straight party basis. For this reason a bipartisan agreement was reached whereby each party would put up a slate limited to 118 names. The assumption was that if Party A carried the state all of its 118 candidates would be swept into office, and the top 59 candidates on Party B's slate would fill the remaining places in the legislature. This is not a "winner-take-all" formula but rather a "winner-take-all-but-one-third" approach. Its consequence would be to disrupt Illinois' legislative politics—especially the status of the second-place party—and the result would clearly motivate other states to present judicially-acceptable districting plans before 1966.

Second Chambers

The Supreme Court turned from general principles to specific cases when, on June 15, 1964, it handed down judgments on the districts of six states: Alabama, New York, Colorado, Maryland, Virginia, and Delaware. Interestingly, four of these six dealt with apportionment plans that had been drawn up after March 1962, and hence purported to meet the standards implicit in Baker v. Carr. In Reynolds v. Sims and five companion cases the Justices sought to resolve several questions that had been left outstanding.[30] The Court ruled, most significantly, that "the seats in both houses of a bicameral legislature must be apportioned on a population basis." Chief Justice Warren, speaking

[30] Reynolds v. Sims, 84 S. Ct. 1362 (Alabama); WMCA v. Lorenzo, 84 S. Ct. 1418 (New York); Maryland Committee for Fair Representation v. Tawes, 84 S. Ct. 1442 (Maryland); Davis v. Mann, 84 S. Ct. 1453 (Virginia); Roman v. Sincock, 84 S. Ct. 1462 (Delaware); Lucas v. 44th General Assembly of Colorado, 84 S. Ct. 1472 (Colorado). Justice Harlan dissented in all six cases; he was joined by Justices Clark and Stewart in the New York and Colorado cases.

for majorities that ranged from 8-to-1 to 6-to-3 depending on the case, rejected the theory that each state was a miniature "federal" system and could thus base one of its legislative chambers on local governmental units rather than population. And in the Colorado case the Court ruled that even if a majority of a state's voters approved an apportionment plan in an initiative or a referendum, such a scheme would be held invalid if it failed to base districts on population.

Chief Justice Warren rehearsed most of the arguments that Justice Brennan had made for the Court in *Baker v. Carr* two years earlier. "Legislators represent people, not trees or acres," he said. "Legislators are elected by voters, not farms or cities or economic interests."[31] When one district is ten times the size of another and both are assigned but a single representative, it is as if both districts were equal in population but the voters in one were handed a sheaf of ten ballots and told they were specially privileged to cast them all. "It would appear extraordinary," Warren remarked, "to suggest that a state could be constitutionally permitted to enact a law providing that certain of the state's voters could vote two, five, or ten times for their legislative representatives, while voters living elsewhere could vote only once."[32] The constitutional ground remained as before: equal protection under the Fourteenth Amendment. But that guarantee was now extended to a citizen's voting rights for both chambers of his state's legislature.

The effect of the *Reynolds v. Sims* group of decisions is to call for a re-examination of state bicameralism. Each state save Nebraska has had two chambers since its admission to the Union—and some states had them even before that time—and the practice has been for one to give disproportionately greater representation to sparsely settled areas. Even if both chambers of a state legislature discriminated in favor of rural backwaters, as most have done, one was usually rather more favorable to the hinterland than was the other. A frequently heard justification was that just as the United States Senate represented the states in the Congress, so one state chamber might give representation to counties or townships or some other governmental units regardless of what their populations might be. Many of the states, for example, provided that each of their counties must have a minimum of one seat

[31] *Reynolds v. Sims. op. cit.*, p. 1382.
[32] *Ibid.*

in one of the chambers no matter how many people might reside within its borders.

Yet even if larger counties had multiple representatives the one-legislator-per-county minimum would give rural areas disproportionate power. The reason for this, quite simply, is that legislatures would have to have memberships approaching 1,000 if the smallest counties were to retain their spokesmen and if the chamber were at the same time apportioned on population. An extreme case: if Nevada County in California (population, 20,911) kept its one member, Los Angeles County would have to have 300 members, and the legislature as a whole would number almost 800. At all events, the Supreme Court was not prepared to take counties or other intrastate units seriously:

> Political subdivisions of states—counties, cities, or whatever—never were and never have been considered as sovereign entities. Rather, they have been traditionally regarded as subordinate governmental instrumentalities created by the states to assist in the carrying out of state governmental functions.[33]

If there was no constitutional foundation for the theory of "miniature federalism," the Court was not prepared to suggest that bicameralism had been rendered purposeless. Those states wishing to retain duplicate debates, hearings, and roll-calls as part of their legislative processes might continue with such an arrangement. Even with equal populations for districts, Chief Justice Warren suggested, "different constituencies can be represented in the two houses":

> One body could be composed of single-member districts while the other could have at least some multi-member districts. The length of terms of the legislators in the separate bodies could differ. The numerical size of the two bodies could be made to differ, even significantly, and the geographical size of districts from which legislators are elected could also be made to differ. And apportionment in one house could be arranged so as to balance off minor inequities in the representation of certain areas in the other house. In summary, these and other factors could be, and are presently in many states, utilized to engender differing complexions and collective attitudes in the two bodies of a state legislature, although both are apportioned substantially on a population basis.[34]

[33] *Ibid.*, p. 1388.
[34] *Ibid.*, p. 1389.

The Compassionate Coloradans

Finally, there was the intriguing question raised in the Colorado case. In the 1962 general election the voters of Colorado, by a margin of 305,700 to 172,725, amended their state's constitution so as to give minimum representation in the state's upper house to certain districts despite their meager populations. Presumably this arrangement was considered equitable by the people of Colorado, or at least by two-thirds of them, for the amendment received a majority in every one of the 63 counties of the state, large as well as small. The voters thus signified their willingness to dilute their own legislative voice and give disproportionate power to rural minorities elsewhere in their state. If this is so, far from indicating "majority tyranny" at the polls, it is an example of the very opposite: a majority agrees to amplify the influence of a minority which stood in danger of being rendered power-less under an apportionment formula based on numbers alone.

The Court, however, was not concerned with the rights of the *mi-nority*—or at least those of rural minorities—but rather with the rights of *individuals*. It declined to acknowledge that there existed any con-stitutional justification for arrangements wherein the political power of some citizens might be greater than that of others. Chief Justice Warren, therefore, put his stress on what would happen to the voter in Denver (population: 493,887) rather than the consequence for the voter in Gilpin County (population: 685):

> An individual's constitutionally protected right to cast an equally weighted ballot cannot be denied even by a vote of a majority of a state's electorate. . . . We hold that the fact that a challenged legisla-tive apportionment was approved by the electorate is without Fed-eral significance, if the scheme adopted failed to satisfy the basic requirements of the Equal Protection clause.[35]

It is a precept of American constitutional law that certain rights exist which a citizen cannot trade, barter, or even give away. These rights, the end-products of a process of historical evolution that is often but dimly understood by those who possess them, express the freedoms upon which the pursuit of the good life depends. It is not inconceivable that there are Americans who, under some circum-

[35] *Lucas v. 44th General Assembly of Colorado, op cit.,* p. 1486.

stances, might be induced to trade away their right to worship, to express their political views, or to maintain domestic privacy. The answer is that citizens of a free society need these rights—whether they know it or not—for their full development. Without such guarantees they will never make the most of the potentialities that are inherently theirs. The Colorado decision is, essentially, an example of Rousseau's theory of the "General Will" applied in practice. The Supreme Court admonished the people of Colorado for their shortsightedness and, in invalidating their majority vote, "forced them to be free." Those of the 305,700 citizens who supported a measure diluting their own legislative effectivenesss did not realize the harm they were thereby rendering themselves. Thus the Court, in voiding a referendum, was informing the majority of its own interests—interests that on Election Day had been imperfectly understood and too easily relinquished.

The Colorado case was unusual in that it was designed, not to protect a minority from the unjust power of the majority—the usual reason for Supreme Court reversals of state acts—but to protect the majority from itself. Had a majority, in an initiative or a referendum, voted to enact a law that would have been oppressive to some racial or religious minority in the state, there would have been little reason to comment on the Court's invalidation of such an enactment. But here was a majority that had embarked on a course of self-mutilation—an instance of the way in which democracy can be used to destroy its own foundations.

Majorities, Minorities, and Individuals

On June 22, 1964, the Court handed down a further group of nine decisions invalidating apportionment schemes in Connecticut, Florida, Idaho, Illinois, Iowa, Michigan, Ohio, Oklahoma, and Washington.[36] In all of these cases but one the districting arrangements for both

[36] These cases were all reported in Memorandum Decisions: *Swann v. Adams,* 84 S. Ct. 1904 (Florida); *Meyers v. Thigpen,* 84 S. Ct. 1905 (Washington); *Nolan v. Rhodes,* 84 S. Ct. 1906 (Ohio); *Williams v. Moss,* 84 S. Ct. 1907 (Oklahoma); *Germano v. Kerner,* 84 S. Ct. 1908 (Illinois); *Marshall v. Hare,* 84 S. Ct. 1912 (Michigan); *Hearne v. Smylie,* 84 S. Ct. 1917 (Idaho); *Pinney v. Butterworth,* 84 S. Ct. 1918 (Connecticut); *Hill v. David,* 84 S. Ct. 1918 (Iowa). Justice Harlan dissented in all nine cases.

houses of state legislatures were declared unconstitutional. (The Ohio decision invalidated only the apportionment formula of its lower chamber.) The Michigan case applied the Colorado principle once again, and a districting plan that had been approved by popular referendum was voided.

Thus by the end of the 1963-1964 term, the Supreme Court had invalidated the districts of 29 of the 99 state legislative houses of the nation. In doing this the Justices set fairly clear guidelines as to what they would and would not find acceptable. And they also made plain that their concern was with the voting rights of *individuals,* in particular with the rights of those citizens who happened to reside in underrepresented districts. "The fact that an individual lives here or there," Chief Justice Warren wrote in *Reynolds v. Sims,* "is not a legitimate reason for overweighting or diluting the efficacy of his vote."[37]

This should be stressed, because most reporting on legislative apportionment—for example, in the *Congressional Quarterly,* the *New York Times,* by the National Municipal League—has been prone to classify legislatures in terms of the percentage of a state's population that can elect a majority of each chamber's members. For instance, of New York's 58 senators, a majority could be elected by the voters who happen to live in districts comprising only 36.9 percent of the state's population. According to this method of analysis, minority rule prevails in New York and virtually every other state. In actual fact, of course, the voters living in the underpopulated districts that elect 30 of New York's 58 senators do not necessarily comprise a homogeneous or cohesive bloc. What can be said is that one *party* or another can benefit through inequitable districting. In the case of the New York Senate the aggregate statewide vote for candidates for that legislative house was remarkably even in 1962: 2,715,000 votes were cast for Republican candidates, while Democrats received 2,712,000. But the Republicans ended up with 33 of the 58 Senate seats, the Democrats with only 25. This, then, was not so much a case of "minority rule" as of a bare majority at the polls being translated into a substantial majority at the state capitol.

The 29 legislative apportionments invalidated by the Court in June

[37] *Reynolds v. Sims., op. cit.,* p. 1384.

1964 had been so designed, the National Municipal League reported, that the following percentages of the various states' populations were able to elect majorities in their respective chambers:[38]

State	Lower Chamber	Upper Chamber
Idaho	44.0	16.6
Michigan	44.0	29.0
Maryland	42.3	14.2
Virginia	40.5	41.1
Illinois	39.9	28.7
Alabama	37.9	27.6
Washington	35.3	33.9
New York	34.7	36.9
Colorado	32.1	29.8
Oklahoma	29.5	24.5
Ohio	28.4	—
Delaware	27.6	29.9
Florida	26.9	15.2
Iowa	26.9	35.2
Connecticut	12.0	32.0

The percentages for Idaho's and Michigan's lower houses were not egregiously out of line with the principle of majority rule. While the counties containing 44 percent of the population might elect a majority bloc, the odds are that this would be a paper majority rather than a real one. In other words the real majorities in these two chambers— in particular, the party majorities—would probably have been elected by popular majorities within the electorate.

Yet the principle of majority rule, as has been indicated, has not been the Court's major concern. The "equal protection" clause of the Fourteenth Amendment is designed to provide protection for individuals, not majorities. Therefore the Court looked at the actual size of districts in these 15 states. And for Idaho and Michigan they found distinct disparities in population between the largest and the smallest lower-chamber districts:

	Largest District	Smallest District	Ratio
Idaho	10,384	915	11.4-to-1
Michigan	135,268	34,006	4.0-to-1

[38] Reported in *Congressional Quarterly Weekly Report*, June 19, 1964, p. 1219.

TABLE 4. *Houses of State Legislatures: Value of Vote in Smallest District Compared to One Vote in Largest*[a]

(Lower house in roman; upper house in italic)

State[b]	Vote Value Smallest District (Largest = 1)	State[b]	Vote Value Smallest District (Largest = 1)	State[b]	Vote Value Smallest District (Largest = 1)
Vermont	934.0	Missouri	13.5	Wisconsin	4.5
Connecticut	424.0*	Montana	12.6	*Indiana*	*4.4*
California	*422.0*	*Michigan*	*12.4*	*South Dakota*	*4.3*
Nevada	*223.5*	Delaware	12.2*	Virginia	4.3*
New Hampshire	222.1	Minnesota	12.0	California	4.2
New Mexico	*140.0*	Idaho	11.4*	Michigan	4.0*
Idaho	*102.1**	*Pennsylvania*	*10.7*	*Minnesota*	*3.8*
Georgia	99.0	*Illinois*	*10.6**	*West Virginia*	*3.4*
Rhode Island	*96.9*	*Wyoming*	*9.8*	South Carolina	3.4
Montana	*88.4*	*Iowa*	*9.0**	North Dakota	3.2
Arizona	84.8	*North Dakota*	*8.9*	Texas	3.1
West Virginia	57.5	*Mississippi*	*8.9*	*Wisconsin*	*3.8*
Rhode Island	39.1	*Texas*	*8.4*	*Maine*	*2.8*
Maryland	*31.7**	Louisiana	8.3	*Virginia*	*2.6**
Pennsylvania	31.1	Colorado	8.1	Wyoming	2.6
Utah	27.9	*Connecticut*	*8.1**	New Jersey	2.6
Oklahoma	*26.4**	*Louisiana*	*7.9*	*New Hampshire*	*2.6*
Florida	*26.4**	Mississippi	7.4	*Arkansas*	*2.5*
South Carolina	*25.1*	*Washington*	*7.3**	Alaska	2.5
Florida	23.3*	*Colorado*	*7.3*	*Massachusetts*	*2.3*
Nevada	22.0	*Utah*	*6.9*	*Oregon*	*2.3*
Kansas	21.4	Arkansas	6.4	*New York*	*2.2**
New York	21.0*	*North Carolina*	*6.0*	Tennessee	2.2
Alabama	*19.8**	*Hawaii*	*5.9*	Hawaii	2.2
Alaska	*19.1*	Maryland	5.8*	Kentucky	2.1
New Jersey	*19.1*	*Vermont*	*5.5*	Oregon	2.1
North Carolina	18.2	Maine	5.5	*Ohio*	*2.1*
Iowa	16.8*	Indiana	5.4	*Kentucky*	*1.9*
New Mexico	15.5*	Arizona	5.3	*Nebraska*	*1.7*
Delaware	*15.5**	Illinois	4.7*	*Missouri*	*1.7*
Ohio	14.5*	Alabama	4.7*	*Tennessee*	*1.6*
Oklahoma	14.0*	South Dakota	4.7	*Georgia*	*1.5*
Massachusetts	13.8	Washington	4.6*	*Kansas*	*1.3*

[a] Source, *Congressional Quarterly Weekly Report*, June 19, 1964. Value-of-Vote ratios are based on districts as constituted on June 16, 1964. Asterisks indicate districting held unconstitutional by Supreme Court decisions on June 15 and 22, 1964.

[b] Two houses for each state, except Nebraska.

Thus one Idaho citizen had one vote, while another had the equivalent of eleven votes, and one Michigan citizen had one vote, while another had what amounted to four votes.

In their decisions of June 15 and 22, 1964, the Justices invalidated apportionments ranging from Connecticut's lower house, where the ratio between most-favored and least-favored citizen was 424 to 1, to New York's upper house, where it was 2.2 to 1. As Table 4 shows, most of the 99 chambers contain sets of districts with one having a population at least double that of another. If New York's ratio of 2.2 to 1 was found discriminatory, this suggests that only the nine houses with ratios smaller than New York's can at this time be assumed to fall within the range of equitable districting. The other 90 apportionments are sufficiently removed from the principle of "one man, one vote" to be prima facie unconstitutional. As of mid-July, 1964, then, every state, including Nebraska,[39] would have to revise its districting arrangements —so long as the Supreme Court's decisions were the final word on the apportionment question.

Congress and the Constitution

In the summer and early fall of 1964 an overweening amount of congressional time and energy was devoted to an assault on *Reynolds v. Sims.* The attack's real object was, of course, the Supreme Court. As we noted earlier, the school desegregation decision of 1954 had upset the sensibilities of southern congressmen; subsequent decisions had persuaded many of their colleagues that the Court was against religion, in favor of obscenity, and not opposed to letting criminals roam the streets. With these more emotion-laden issues available, it is curious that apportionment became the occasion for attempted censure. Perhaps the only explanation is that *Reynolds v. Sims* happened to come along near the end of a disquieting Court term and just as the 1964 political campaign was going into high gear.

The sequence of events on Capitol Hill was confusing and complex. By a vote of 218 to 175 the House rushed through a bill to place state legislative districting outside federal court jurisdiction. The Senate was

[39] On July 15, 1964, a three-judge federal court ordered Nebraska to reapportion its unicameral legislature; it indicated, however, that this action might be postponed until the 1966 election. Nebraska's smallest district stood at 21,703 and its largest at 36,393; a ratio of 1 to 1.7.

unwilling to go along with the House bill (in one test only 21 votes were mustered for it), but sentiment was strong for doing *something* about the matter. After a debate of filibuster proportions, a "sense of Congress" resolution was passed by a vote of 44 to 38, asking district court judges considering apportionment cases to allow the 1964 elections for state legislatures to be held with the districts then in existence. The judges were also asked to allow the legislatures, when they convened in 1965, up to six months to draw new constituency boundaries. Finally, if the legislatures failed to come up with reforms by mid 1965, the judges were advised to do the reapportionment themselves.

This moderate expression had so little in common with the House bill that the conference committee simply decided that compromise action was impossible in the great push for adjournment. If this seemed an anticlimax after a debate that had dominated the last months of the 88th Congress, the issue was far from closed. Leaders in both houses promised to initiate a constitutional amendment as soon as the 89th Congress opened: the most likely proposal would permit one house of a bicameral state legislature to be based on criteria other than population, thus overriding *Reynolds v. Sims*. The arrangement would be permitted, however, only if a majority of a state's voters gave approval in a referendum.

"No" votes from only 34 senators can keep the amendment from going to the states for ratification. And even if a two-thirds vote is mustered in both House and Senate, the amendment, to pass, must secure majorities in at least 75 of the 99 state legislative chambers. If the proposal does reach the states, there will be, as one senator put it, the irony of having "the rotten boroughs decide whether they should continue to be rotten."

The issue of state apportionments will continue to be a vexing problem for several years, but the principle of "one man, one vote" has been effectively raised. City councils, county boards, and even the conventions and committees of state party organizations will be scrutinized with respect to their representative character. Paradoxically, the institution that has so far accepted its reform with the best grace and least resistance has been the national House of Representatives. But even here there is much unfinished business to attend to.

3

Political Cartography

THE CONSTITUTION PRESCRIBES that "each house shall be the judge of the elections, returns, and qualifications of its own members. . . ." The House of Representatives has the power to decide in what manner its members shall be elected and what determines a legitimate constituency for such election. From time to time throughout its history, the House has legislated on this subject, although the pattern has been sporadic both in intention and effect.

The constitutional provision was simply that each state was to receive a specific number of representatives, based on the population of the state. The framers were notably silent on how these men were to be elected, other than to say that the franchise must be extended to all qualified to vote for the lower house of the state legislature. Many of the states, therefore, elected all of their representatives on a statewide, or at-large, basis. What happened, of course, was that in states where one party had a comfortable statewide majority it carried the entire congressional delegation. As a remedy for this "winner take all" arrangement, the Apportionment Act of 1842 was passed by the Congress. The statute declared that congressmen must "be elected by districts composed of contiguous territory equal in number to the number of Representatives to which said state may be entitled, no one district electing more than one Representative."[1] In other words, the map of each state had to be divided into distinct geographic constituencies, each having its own congressman. The districts had to be contiguous, but the law did not stipulate that they had to be equal in population.

[1] 5 Stat. 491 (1842).

The 1842 Act was a major step toward proportioning representation to the distribution of votes.[2] This may be illustrated in contemporary terms by pointing out that there would be no Republican congressman from Missouri or Virginia, nor would there be a Democrat from Ohio, were those states to elect all their representatives at large. The requirement of districts gives the minority party at least the chance to elect one or two candidates if its supporters are strategically concentrated in certain parts of the state. But the Act of 1842 is no longer law of the land. Its provisions were not incorporated in subsequent reapportionment acts. As a result, at-large districts are again in evidence. In the 88th Congress, 17 of the 435 representatives were elected on a statewide basis. However, there is little likelihood that this number will increase. For the district system is well-entrenched, and at-large elections are usually temporary measures adopted because a state legislature cannot immediately agree on how to alter the map to take account of the addition or loss of a district.

In 1872, the Congress directed that all districts should contain "as nearly as practicable an equal number of inhabitants"; and, in 1901, it stated that districts should be composed of "compact territory."[3] But the requirement for equal population was dropped in the 1901 Act, and the rule on compactness was not renewed after 1911. Indeed, since 1911, the subsequent apportionment acts have omitted what many consider the basic trinity of equitable representation: districts that are contiguous, compact, and of equal size. Efforts have been made from time to time to reinstate these provisions, but with a notable lack of success.

[2] The term "proportionate representation" and its variants will be used frequently throughout this chapter and its meaning should be made clear. It will not refer to the method of election commonly called Proportional Representation, the electoral method under which the voter marks his preferential choices among a slate of candidates. Rather, it will be used to postulate a hypothetical situation wherein the number of congressmen a party contributes to a state delegation corresponds to the proportion of votes that party received in all the congressional contests throughout the state. Thus, if a state's delegation contains 10 representatives, a party receiving 60 percent of the statewide congressional vote would get six of the seats. No proposal is being made here that some form of Proportional Representation be adopted so as to achieve this result in practice. The purpose is to employ an analytical standard that will help to show the workings of the single-member district system.

[3] 17 Stat. 28 (1872) and 31 Stat. 733 (1901). For a general summary of legislation see, Emanuel Celler, "Congressional Apportionment—Past, Present, and Future," Law and Contemporary Problems, Vol. 17 (Spring 1952), pp. 268-75.

There is one other question that cannot, because of its technical complexity, be considered here. This is the arithmetic method of deciding how the 435 congressional seats will be apportioned among the states following each Census. This is by no means a simple matter. The proponents of the "major fractions" procedure, in force between 1911 and 1941, have not yet made their peace with the supporters of the "equal proportions" method, now being used.[4] The controversy is over where the cutoff point is to be for each state. The average size of a congressional district, in national terms, was 410,481 persons according to the 1960 Census returns. How many seats, for example, was West Virginia to be allotted? It had a population of 1,860,421 and was given five seats, averaging only 372,084 in numbers. Contrast this with Arkansas, having 1,786,272 people and receiving four seats, each with an average population of 446,568. The cutoff point between four and five seats, then, was somewhere between 1,786,272 and 1,860,421. A few thousand more people gave West Virginia a fifth seat. The stakes are real in the apportioning process and a state can gain or lose a congressman by a hairbreadth. Nevertheless, the alternative methods are so technical that Congress has long since ceased debating the issue. This is one decision, perhaps the only one, that has been left to the mathematicians.

The Single-Member District

Dividing a state into congressional districts and permitting the residents of each district to elect a representative seems a simple and sensible arrangement. It is sensible, and there is no doubt that it will be continued into the foreseeable future. But the single-member district is far from simple in its electoral consequences. Not only can districts be manipulated through gerrymandering, but slight shifts in voting behavior on the part of citizens, as Table 5 shows, can produce strikingly disproportionate results. For example, it took only an increase of 7 percent in the Indiana Democrats' share of the statewide two-party vote to raise their strength in the state's congressional delegation by 55 per-

[4] See Walter F. Willcox, "Last Words on the Apportionment Problem" and Laurence F. Schmeckebier, "The Method of Equal Proportions," both in *Law and Contemporary Problems, ibid.,* pp. 290-301, 302-13.

cent. In Connecticut, a gain of 16 percent in the share of the vote coincided with a shift from one Democratic representative to five. In all these states, a gain of 1 percent in votes led to a gain in representatives of at least 2 percent (as in California), and as high as 5 percent (as in Connecticut).

TABLE 5. *Changes in Democratic Statewide Vote Compared to Changes in Democratic Congressional Seats, Selected States, 1954–58*[a]

State	Number of Seats in U. S. Congress	Percentage Democratic Statewide Vote			Percentage Democratic Congressmen in State Delegation		
		1954	1958	Change 1954–58	1954	1958	Change 1954–58
Connecticut	5[b]	38	54	16	20	100	80
Maryland	7	54	66	12	57	100	43
Iowa	8	41	50	9	0	50	50
California	30	52	60	8	37	53	16
Indiana	11	47	54	7	18	73	55
Kansas	6	43	50	7	0	50	50
Ohio	23	46	51	5	26	39	13

[a] Source, U. S. Bureau of the Census, *Congressional District Data Book, Districts of the 87th Congress*, a supplement to *Statistical Abstract of the United States* (1961).
[b] A sixth Connecticut district is on an at-large basis.

The reason for such disproportionate harvests is obvious. The voters who, between 1954 and 1958, shifted from Republican to Democratic allegiance were distributed in several marginal districts. In 1954, they had voted Republican and theirs were the strategic ballots that elected Republican candidates. In 1958, by shifting to the Democratic column, they turned the scales in the other direction. Where independent-minded voters hold the balance of power, as they did in these competitive states, a slight change in one party's fortunes can produce a congressional windfall. Quite clearly, from the congressional point of view 1958 was a "Democratic year" and in that election a strategic number of independents shifted away from the Republicans.

The single-member district gives the appearance of functioning under an arithmetic logic of its own. "A net shift of one percent of the electorate from one party to the other," Robert Dahl concluded, "will result in a net gain of about 2.5 percent of the House seats for the benefitted party."[5] Over the long run, this tendency seems to be operative, as shown in Table 6 giving data for the period 1942-62. During those years, the proportion of popular votes received by the parties varied

TABLE 6. *Relationship of Party's National Congressional Vote to Seats Won in the U. S. House of Representatives, Democrats and Republicans, 1942–62*[a]

(In Percentages)

Year	National Vote	Seats Won	Difference
DEMOCRATS:			
1942	47.7	51.2	+3.5
1944	51.8	56.0	+4.2
1946	45.3	43.4	−1.9
1948	53.3	60.6	+7.3
1950	50.3	54.0	+3.7
1952	50.2	48.8	−1.4
1954	52.8	53.3	+0.5
1956	51.3	53.8	+2.5
1958	56.4	64.9	+8.5
1960	54.9	60.1	+5.2
1962	52.2	59.7	+7.5
REPUBLICANS:			
1942	52.3	48.8	−3.5
1944	48.2	44.0	−4.2
1946	54.7	56.6	+1.9
1948	46.7	39.4	−7.3
1950	49.7	46.0	−3.7
1952	49.8	51.2	+1.4
1954	47.2	46.7	−0.5
1956	48.7	46.2	−2.5
1958	43.6	35.1	−8.5
1960	45.1	39.9	−5.2
1962	47.8	40.3	−7.5

[a] Sources, U. S. Bureau of the Census, *Statistical Abstract of the United States, 1962*, Eighty-third Edition (1962), p. 361; and Republican National Committee, *The 1962 Election* (1963), p. 1.

[5] Robert Dahl, *A Preface to Democratic Theory* (University of Chicago Press, 1956), p. 146. See also James C. March, "Party Legislative Representation as a Function of Election Results," *Public Opinion Quarterly*, Vol. 21 (Winter 1957-58), p. 523.

within a range of 12.8 percentage points (43.6 percent to 56.4 percent) while the proportion of seats won was within a 29.8 point range (35.1 percent to 64.9 percent). Nevertheless, there are some interesting exceptions to the general case. In two instances, the party winning a majority of the popular vote failed to secure a majority of the House seats (1942, the Republicans; 1952, the Democrats). This is especially striking in the case of the Republicans, who gained 52.3 percent of the vote in 1942, but, only 48.8 percent of the seats. That result should be contrasted with 1962, where the Democratic vote was 52.2 percent and that party ended up with 59.7 percent of the seats in the House. The point is that this tendency is uneven in its operation. Most important, it discriminates in favor of the Democrats, and for the straightforward reason that they pick up several dozen seats in the southern states with a relative handful of votes. Thus, when the Republicans did have a clear majority of the popular votes in 1946, their increment of seats was much lower than an equivalent Democratic gain would have brought. Even so, the Democrats' record is not consistent. Between 1954 and 1956, for example, that party's vote fell from 52.8 percent to 51.3 percent (1.5 points), yet its share of the House seats rose from 53.3 percent to 53.8 percent (0.5 points). Nevertheless, despite all these exceptions and qualifications, study of the relation between votes received and seats won does reveal that the latter percentage by and large climbs at a faster rate than the former. It will probably be necessary to adjust Dahl's 2.5 to 1 ratio for each party, although there is no indication that presidential election years function much differently from mid-term elections.

The rule that seats won can be disproportionate to votes cast may be undermined by ensuring that the independent voters are concentrated in a few districts rather than being widely distributed throughout the state. This may be seen from Table 5. While 52 percent of the California voters supported Democrats in 1954, Democratic candidates nevertheless captured only 11 of the 30 seats in the state's delegation. By the same token, when 51 percent of the 1958 votes cast in Ohio went to Democrats, only nine Democratic congressmen ended up in a delegation of 23. These were disproportions of a negative sort, so far as the Democrats were concerned, and they resulted not from chance but from design. In both California and Ohio, Republican legislatures had sought to ensure that Democratic votes would be distributed so they counted for as little as possible, and this had worked for California in 1954 and Ohio in 1958. But when the Democratic proportion of the California vote rose to 60 percent in 1958, voters were distributed well enough to carry 16 of the state's 30 districts. Gerrymandering, then, can stem a rising stream effectively, but it cannot hold back a raging flood. Considering that most elections are not of flood proportions, the manipulation of district boundaries continues to be an important political tool.

Varieties of Gerrymandering

There is a good deal of casual discussion of gerrymandering but very few people actually understand how it works. A Pennsylvania politician once explained how the Republican legislature in his state rearranged the contours of a district so that it would remain safe for the incumbent:

> First they took away some Democratic stuff. Next they added more Democrats than they took away. And finally they gave him some new Republican stuff. But the net result was just a small Democratic gain, and the district's still safe for a Republican.[6]

Gerrymandering, in short, is the art of political cartography. The "stuff" here referred to is actually people or, more accurately, voters who can be expected to support one party fairly consistently. By giving some attention to the past voting records of ward and precinct subdivisions it is possible to identify Democratic blocks in the cities or Republican townships in the countryside. The party controlling the state legislature will draw up many preliminary maps before it decides on the one that will most redound to its electoral favor. Like counters in a game, sections of territory are moved around in the redistricting process. The final product is often a map with one or more elongated districts meandering across the state, picking up Democratic or Republican "stuff" in hopes of securing enough votes to carry the seat for the party fortunate enough to grasp the cartographer's pen.

[6] Quoted in Chalmers Roberts, "The Donkey, the Elephant, and the Gerrymander," *The Reporter*, September 16, 1952.

If the aim of gerrymandering is for one party to obtain the maximum voting advantage at the other's expense, there are several methods by which this can be done. In each, the gerrymandering party (henceforward to be called Party A) intends to make the votes of the opposition (Party B) as ineffective as possible. One method is for Party A to set up a district in which Party B will have "excess" votes—that is, considerably more votes will be cast for Party B's candidate than he needs to win. A second method is to create a district where Party B's "wasted" votes—those cast for a predictable loser—will be increased. And the third is to design a district so that Party A's "effective" votes will be increased—usually by putting its own known followers into small districts compared to much larger districts for Party B's known followers.

Excess Votes

Winning a district by a comfortable majority is one thing; winning by an overcomfortable majority is a luxury that a party can well do without. A candidate who wins with 90 percent of the votes cast in his district has votes far in excess of what is needed for victory. More important, there will be other candidates of his party, in neighboring districts, who may lose their races by quite small margins. It goes without saying that they could have put his excess votes to good use in their contests. The practice of the gerrymandering Party A, therefore, is to concentrate the supporters of Party B in a few selected districts. Party B is allowed to win these seats, but at the price of very large majorities. In theory, Party A would arrange to carry all its seats with comfortable majorities while Party B's victories would be calculated landslides.

In a five-district state, for example, Party A could win four of the seats even though it had fewer votes on a statewide basis than did Party B. Table 7 details such a hypothetical case. It is an extreme case purposely set up to provide a striking illustration of how this type of gerrymander works. Party A, receiving 48 percent of the vote, managed to obtain 80 percent of the seats in the congressional delegation. Party B, with 52 percent of the votes, won only a single seat. The key to this outcome lies in the proportion of the party's votes that fell into the excess category.[7] Of Party B's votes 30.7 percent were excess votes, but Party A's excess votes came to only 25 percent of its total. This may seem a small difference but it is crucial in determining how many congressmen each party will elect. Moreover, it is not difficult to see how Party B's excess votes in the fifth district would have been welcomed by its candidates in the other four districts. It goes without saying that it was Party A's intention to ensure that this did not occur.

Large concentrations of excess votes are not always to be attributed

TABLE 7. *Gerrymandering to Increase the Opposition's Excess Votes, a Hypothetical Case*

(Gerrymandering party is A; opposition party is B)

Districts Won	Winner's Votes	Loser's Votes	Winner's Majority (Percent)	Winner's Excess Votes
BY PARTY A:				
1st	115,000	85,000	57.5	29,999
2nd	115,000	85,000	57.5	29,999
3rd	115,000	85,000	57.5	29,999
4th	115,000	85,000	57.5	29,999
	460,000	340,000		119,996
BY PARTY B:				
5th	180,000	20,000	90.0	159,999

Summary	Party A		Party B	
	Number	Percent	Number	Percent
Congressmen elected	4		1	
Total votes cast by party	480,000		520,000	
Party's percent statewide vote		48.0		52.0
Excess votes	119,996		159,999	
Percent excess party votes		25.0		30.7

[7] "Excess votes" are defined here as those exceeding the minimum number needed to defeat an opponent. In actual practice, of course, a party likes to have a comfortable margin of safety. However, for purposes of simplicity and uniformity it is best to start counting excess votes at the point where a one-vote victory has been achieved. The bias in this method should be borne in mind.

to the deftness of the mapmakers. Many cities contain large "natural" aggregations of Democrats and they inevitably produce top-heavy majorities for at least some of that party's candidates. While Democratic legislatures occasionally have tried to redistribute their excess votes, they seldom succeed. For it is not really feasible to take Democratic votes in the heart of a city and join them in a single district with Republican suburban votes. A district running from slum to suburb as a rule would cut across other urban districts, and this is regarded as violating one of the few rules of the gerrymandering game. Therefore, in the North at least, Republicans can use gerrymanders to better advantage. Until Democratic voters distribute themselves more widely, Democratic legislators are compelled to cut their losses in other ways.

Wasted Votes

Because it is not always possible to impose excessive majorities on the opposition party, an alternative type of gerrymander is often used. Here the goal is to waste as many as possible of the opposition's votes by arranging that they be cast for losing candidates. Wasted votes, in other words, are votes cast for a candidate who is ultimately defeated.

An eight-district state is used for illustrative purposes in Table 8. Here, however, gerrymandering Party A has a majority—52 percent—of the statewide votes, and thus has at least a theoretical claim to a majority of the seats in the delegation. But in spite of its fairly small statewide majority of only 52 percent, it has managed in this case to obtain seven of the eight districts for its candidates. This was accomplished by so distributing Party B's votes that in all except one district they would be in the minority. Thus, over 80 percent of Party B's electoral support was thrown behind losing candidates. It should be noted that Party A's excess vote is much higher in this case than Party B's, 21.2 percent compared to 5.3 percent. But that is a price cheerfully and inevitably exacted for winning extra seats by this type of gerrymander.

Effective Votes and Unequal Districts

The effective votes are those remaining after the first two classes—the excess and wasted votes—have been subtracted. If it is the aim of

Party A to increase as much as possible the wasted or excess votes of Party B, by the same token its goal is to secure for itself as many effective votes as possible.

The two illustrations used in Tables 7 and 8 have hypothesized districts of equal size. In both cases, all districts in the state had exactly 200,000 votes cast in them, implying that they were also identical in total population.

TABLE 8. *Gerrymandering to Increase the Opposition's Wasted Votes, a Hypothetical Case*

(Gerrymandering party is A; opposition party is B)

Districts Won	Winner's Votes	Loser's Votes	*Winner's Majority (Percent)*	Winner's Excess Votes
BY PARTY A:				
1st	110,000	90,000	*55*	19,999
2nd	110,000	90,000	*55*	19,999
3rd	110,000	90,000	*55*	19,999
4th	110,000	90,000	*55*	19,999
5th	110,000	90,000	*55*	19,999
6th	110,000	90,000	*55*	19,999
7th	110,000	90,000	*55*	19,999
	770,000	630,000		179,991
BY PARTY B:				
8th	120,000	80,000	*60*	39,999

Summary	Party A		Party B	
	Number	*Percent*	Number	*Percent*
Congressmen elected	7		1	
Total votes cast by party	850,000		750,000	
Party's percent statewide vote		*52.0*		*48.0*
Wasted votes	80,000		630,000	
Percent wasted party votes		*9.4*		*84.0*
Excess votes	179,991		39,999	
Percent excess party votes		*21.2*		*5.3*
Effective votes	590,009		80,001	
Percent effective party votes		*69.4*		*10.7*

Gerrymandering is entirely possible when districts are equal in size, as these examples have suggested. Indeed, the artistry of the political cartographer is put to its highest test when he must work with constituencies of equal population. At such times, his skills can be compared to those of a surgeon, for both work under fixed and arduous rules. However, if the mapmaker is free to allocate varying populations to different districts, then the butcher's cleaver replaces the scalpel; and the results reflect sharply the difference in the method of operation. For then Party A can multiply Party B's excess votes simply by cramming more and more of its supporters into a single district.

A state with 2.8 million residents will be given a congressional delegation with seven members. If the seven districts were equitably drawn, each one would contain 400,000 people or some figure approximating that norm. However, the gerrymandering party may have other considerations than equity in mind as it lays down district boundaries. Thus, in Table 9's hypothetical case, over half the state's population, the part likely to support Party B, was squeezed into two of seven districts. And the remainder, which can be counted upon to elect Party

TABLE 9. *Gerrymandering Unequal Districts, a Hypothetical Case*
(Gerrymandering party is A; opposition party is B)

Districts Won	Population	Percent Population Norm[a]
BY PARTY A:		
1st	150,000	37.5
2nd	225,000	56.2
3rd	300,000	75.0
4th	175,000	43.8
5th	450,000	111.2
Total, 5 Party A districts	1,300,000	
Average, 1st–5th districts	260,000	64.7
BY PARTY B:		
6th	700,000	175.0
7th	800,000	200.0
Total, 2 Party B districts	1,500,000	
Average, 6th–7th districts	750,000	188.0

a Population norm per district = 400,000.

A's candidates, was spread out among five constituencies. This means that an average citizen living in a district won by Party B must share his congressman with 750,000 of his neighbors, while the average individual residing in a district won by Party A has to share his with only 260,000. The point is not so much that Party A wants to underrepresent certain kinds of people, although this motive plays an important secondary role. Rather, Party A wants to ensure the election of its own candidates, and it can do this by giving them constituencies containing a small number of voters whose support can be relied upon. Were all the districts compelled to be closer to the norm of 400,000, then many of Party B's adherents would have to be relocated in what is now Party A territory, thus threatening the safe position of candidates there.

In the examples used earlier, illustrating the uses of excess and wasted votes, at least all citizens had ballots of theoretically equal value. If all districts are the same size, as they were in those cases, then every resident of the state has an equal "share" in his congressman. (Of course, Republican voters may not be very happy about being represented by a Democrat and vice versa.) But if, in the current example, residents of the fourth and sixth districts are compared, it will be seen that the latter has one-fourth as much "share" in a congressman as the former. This means, in effect, that the person living in the fourth district has a vote of four times the value of a person in the sixth. For all congressmen are equal—at least on a roll call in Washington—no matter how many people live in their constituencies back home.

It is sometimes argued that the creation of unequal districts is not actually gerrymandering. This, however, is mainly an aesthetic objection, and is based on the belief that cramming the opposition into a sardine tin is too heavy-handed an operation to be worthy of the mantle of Elbridge Gerry. The point is that gerrymandering is the maneuvering of district boundaries for partisan advantage. The overall aim is to deploy one's own voting support to maximum advantage. By putting opposition voters into large districts and its own followers in small ones, the party controlling the legislature is certainly able to safeguard additional seats. In one sense, this is simply a supplementary way of increasing the opposition's excess votes throughout the state, although that end is achieved differently from the method employed when all

districts are of equal size. At present, most states have districts showing appreciable deviations from their population norms, and such variations in size undoubtedly are playing a role in congressional elections.
The question, then, is whether this is a consequential role.

An attempt at an answer is made here by examining the 1962 congressional voting patterns in three states. This will provide an opportunity
to see how far the various gerrymandering methods—up to now considered only hypothetically—operate in real life.

Gerrymandering at Work: The 1962 Elections

The three types of gerrymandering just described naturally do not
function in isolation from each other. All three varieties may be seen at
work in any election in any state. However, there are significant differences of degree, and these may be seen by examining what happened
in New York, California, and Michigan during the 1962 congressional
elections. The selection of these particular states, it should be emphasized, stems from the fact that they depict in a graphic way the character and consequences of gerrymandering. No claim can be made that
the three are typical of the other 47 states. Indeed, at this time there
can only be speculation on whatever patterns exist on a national scale.
If and when a thorough survey is undertaken, it will be necessary to
trace the country's electoral experience over an extended period of
years. It cannot be assumed that 1962's voting constitutes a representative sample of what has occurred in the past.

The test employed here is to check on a party's proportion of the
total statewide congressional vote, and how this compared with the
proportion of seats that party secured in the state's congressional delegation. This test is simply a method of investigating the extent of gerrymandering. No suggestion is being made that seats should be proportionate to votes, nor is it likely that they will be while under the system
of single-member districts. And it should not be thought that this form
of analysis is used in order to make a case for electoral reform in the
direction of Proportional Representation. The test is simply a technique
and nothing more.

TABLE 10. *Voting in 1962 Congressional Elections: New York*[a]

(Population norm per district = 409,324)

Districts Won	Winner's Votes			Loser's Wasted Votes	Winner's Majority (*Percent*)	Percent Population Norm
	Total	Effective	Excess			
BY REPUBLICANS:						
2nd	71,648	57,330	14,318	57,329	55.6	91.0
3rd	86,354	59,455	26,899	59,454	59.2	98.0
4th	74,480	54,163	20,317	54,162	57.9	96.2
5th	89,921	66,563	23,358	66,562	57.5	98.5
6th	95,517	55,302	40,215	55,301	63.3	102.0
17th	98,129	45,567	52,562	45,566	68.3	93.4
24th[b]	77,108	46,986	30,122	46,985	59.4	85.6
25th[b]	98,481	62,712	35,769	62,711	61.1	107.1
26th	92,754	59,604	33,150	59,603	60.9	98.3
27th	86,475	62,499	23,976	62,498	58.0	100.0
28th	92,188	51,985	40,203	51,984	63.9	96.8
30th[b]	109,705	56,430	53,275	56,429	64.5	112.6
31st	65,350	42,903	22,447	42,902	60.4	86.3
32nd	76,564	56,989	19,575	56,988	57.3	94.2
33rd[b]	92,370	41,435	50,935	41,434	66.8	101.5
34th[b]	84,239	66,448	17,791	66,447	55.3	103.3
36th	96,925	65,892	31,033	65,891	59.5	100.4
37th	100,634	57,124	43,510	57,123	63.8	100.3
38th[b]	78,821	36,813	42,008	36,812	67.5	93.4
39th[b]	99,713	56,245	43,468	56,244	62.5	106.6
40th	71,979	67,655	4,324	67,654	51.5	106.3
	1,839,355	1,170,100	669,255	1,170,079	60.8	98.7
BY DEMOCRATS:						
1st	84,959	52,795	32,164	52,794	61.7	97.3
7th	80,590	55,660	24,930	55,659	59.1	112.3
8th	104,573	52,969	51,604	52,968	66.4	105.7
9th[b]	85,368	51,519	33,849	51,518	58.4	104.7
10th	86,286	20,557	65,729	20,556	80.8	103.3
11th	56,242	22,462	33,780	22,461	71.5	98.6
12th	103,378	43,785	59,593	43,784	70.2	115.1
13th	115,195	39,215	75,980	39,214	74.6	111.2
14th	53,923	22,257	31,666	22,256	70.8	113.3
15th	55,570	54,693	877	54,692	50.4	85.7
16th[b]	57,395	55,656	1,739	55,655	47.2	86.2
18th[b]	58,712	17,982	40,730	17,981	69.8	105.4
19th[b]	58,823	30,526	28,297	30,525	58.5	108.8
20th	93,994	35,226	58,768	35,225	72.7	107.4
21st	63,891	20,047	43,844	20,046	67.4	88.2
22nd[b]	49,972	14,607	35,365	14,606	70.1	87.9
23rd[b]	66,507	38,831	27,676	38,830	54.0	86.4
29th	124,982	79,828	45,154	79,827	61.0	110.6
35th	74,947	62,760	12,187	62,759	54.4	94.3
41st	93,642	37,446	56,196	37,445	71.4	106.4
	1,568,949	808,821	760,128	808,801	64.6	101.4

Table 10 continued next page

[a] Source, *Congressional Quarterly Weekly Report*, November 16, 1962, p. 2167.

[b] Thirteen districts had a liberal candidate running in addition to the Democrat and Republican. The 100,000 votes won by these Liberal candidates are ignored in computations of this table. In all other districts, the Democrat received the Liberal party endorsement and those Liberal votes are counted in the Democratic column.

TABLE 10. *Continued*

Summary	Republican Party		Democratic Party	
	Number	*Percent*	Number	*Percent*
Congressmen elected	21		20	
Party's percent of total congressmen elected		*51.0*		*49.0*
Total votes cast by party	2,648,156		2,739,028	
Party's percent of statewide vote		*49.2*		*50.8*
Effective votes	1,170,100		808,821	
Percent effective party votes		*44.1*		*29.4*
Excess votes	669,255		760,128	
Percent excess party votes		*25.3*		*27.8*
Wasted votes	808,801		1,170,079	
Percent wasted party votes		*30.6*		*42.8*

New York State

In 1962, the Republicans elected 51 percent of New York's congressmen and, as Table 10 shows, they achieved this result with only 49.2 percent of the two-party vote.[8] How did the minority party manage to win a majority of the seats?

It should be noted at the outset that New York's districts are relatively equal in terms of population. None is below 85 percent or above 115 percent of the state norm for each district. It is true that the average Republican district is 1.3 percent below the norm while the average Democratic district is 1.4 percent above. However, this difference of 2.7 percent is comparatively small when contrasted with other states. If the voters had acted in accord with the plans of the Republican mapmakers, the gap might have been somewhat larger. For the 15th, 16th, and 35th Districts were drawn in the hopes of encompassing Republican majorities within their boundaries. To be on the safe side, these districts were all made small in size, standing respectively at 85.7 percent, 86.2 percent, and 94.3 percent of the norm. However, even the best-made maps are at the mercy of the voters, and in these districts, the voters in 1962 elected Democratic congressmen. Thus, several small districts intended for Republicans ended up in the Democratic column.

[8] In 13 of the 41 district contests, there was a third candidate, usually a Liberal. (In the other 28 races, the Democrat received the Liberal party endorsement and Liberal votes are counted in the Democratic columns.) However, these 13 third-party candidates received less than 100,000 votes in the districts in which they ran, or an average of 1.6 percent of the total vote in those contests. These candidates, therefore, are ignored and all figures refer to the major contestants. In no case did the entry of a Liberal cause a Republican to win by a plurality.

Had the Republicans won those contests, their seats would have averaged 96.7 percent of the state norm and the Democrats would have averaged 103.7 percent—a 7 percent difference, which is appreciable.

Given relative equality of district size, the Republicans managed to ensure that Democratic districts were carried by overlarge majorities. In eight of 20 winning races, the Democrats had from 70.1 to 80.8 percent of the votes; however, in the 21 Republican districts, the winner's highest percentage was 68.3. The average Democratic majority was 64.6 percent,[9] while the Republican figure was a comfortable, but not excessive, 60.8 percent. This contrast can also be seen in the fact that 27.8 percent of the Democratic votes were excess votes compared with 25.3 percent for the Republicans. This actual case thus supports the point made earlier that it takes only a small percentage difference in excess votes to produce significant practical results. It appears, then, that much of the Republican advantage stems from the fact that Democratic votes were concentrated where they ran up overlarge majorities. This was not, to be sure, all the doing of dexterous cartography by Republican hands. For example, in seven districts in Brooklyn and Staten Island (the 10th through the 16th), the Republican vote was only 34.2 percent of the total cast. With such a natural concentration of Democrats, it is hard to see how dissipation of Democratic strength in the area could be prevented.

Probably the most significant Republican gains came from ensuring that sizable numbers of Democratic votes were distributed in districts that nevertheless had Republican majorities. In all except one contest throughout the state, the Democrats wasted over 40,000 votes and most contests saw between 45,000 and 65,000 votes cast for candidates who lost. Thus, wasted Democratic votes ran to 42.8 percent of their total vote, while the Republicans were able to hold their wastage down to 30.6 percent. The Republicans tended to lose to Democratic landslides, thus conserving their strength for strategic use elsewhere. Seen this way, the relation between the Democrat's high excess votes and the Republican's low wasted votes is a reciprocal one.

It is not possible to say how much of the Republican gain in congressional representation may be attributed to Democratic excess votes

[9] The average Democratic majority would have been 67.2 percent if a Liberal had not been running in six of the Democratic districts and if, as would have been likely, the Liberal votes had gone to the Democratic candidate.

as opposed to Democratic wasted votes. The evidence suggests that the latter played a more important role, but there is no way of proving this. In any case, it is clear that district size is a negligible factor in New York. Finally, the winning of 21 districts by the Republicans is not a startling victory, for had their seats been proportionate to their votes they would have won 20. Yet this small difference turned a minority of votes into a congressional majority in the state; for that reason, if no other, New York is worth studying.

California

For California, figures in Table 11 are aimed at answering two questions rather than one. First, how were the Democrats, with 52 percent of the popular vote, able to win 66 percent of the state's 38 congressional seats? Second, with Democrats in control of the legislature, why did they fail to carry an even higher proportion of the districts?

Unlike New York's Republicans, Democrats in the California legislature did not feel obliged to keep districts relatively equal in terms of population. In contrast with New York's range of 15 percent above or below the norm, California's constituencies varied in size from 73 to 142.4 percent of the state population norm. Yet the Democrats were unwilling, or unable, to work the existence of large and small districts to their advantage as much as might be expected. While three of the 25 seats they ultimately won were small (under 85 percent of the norm), five were large (over 115 percent). In contrast, only one of the Republican districts was outside the 15 percent range (the 28th at 142.4 percent). The average Democratic district was 98 percent of the norm and the average Republican was 103.8 percent. This difference of 5.8 percent was probably enough to give the Democrats an electoral advantage. The surprising thing is that the difference, and the consequent advantage it would bring, was not greater.

However, the California Democrats, like all Democrats outside the South, are faced with the problem that Republican strength is not easily concentrated on a map. It is hard to create a heavily populated Republican district with large excess votes because, except for a few well-to-do suburbs, fewer areas seem to attract Republicans en masse than Democrats. It is worth noting that the average majority of both Democratic and Republican winning candidates was 63.9 percent. Indeed,

TABLE 11. *Voting in 1962 Congressional Elections: California*[a]

(Population norm per district=413,611)

Districts Won	Winner's Votes			Loser's Wasted Votes	Winner's Majority (*Percent*)	Percent Population Norm
	Total	Effective	Excess			
BY DEMOCRATS:						
1st	99,740	96,189	3,551	96,188	50.9	129.1
2nd	92,060	49,870	42,190	49,869	64.9	98.3
3rd	135,145	44,771	90,374	44,770	75.1	121.6
4th	56,087	42,837	13,250	42,836	56.7	75.1
5th	55,808	14,321	44,487	14,320	80.4	73.0
7th	84,223	46,106	38,117	46,105	64.6	80.6
8th	95,411	36,632	58,779	36,631	72.3	90.3
9th	76,121	38,867	37,254	38,866	66.2	92.7
15th	95,235	40,864	54,371	40,863	70.0	98.5
16th	107,882	42,230	65,652	42,229	71.9	120.1
17th	71,672	35,349	36,323	35,348	67.0	90.9
18th	91,395	63,893	27,502	63,892	58.9	123.4
19th	77,868	48,232	29,636	48,231	61.8	91.4
21st	70,507	12,951	57,556	12,950	84.5	88.2
22nd	73,729	62,140	11,139	62,139	54.1	95.2
23rd	81,550	45,424	36,126	45,423	64.2	98.7
25th	61,060	52,394	8,666	52,393	53.8	90.0
26th	108,219	49,615	58,604	49,614	68.6	93.9
27th	65,224	58,986	6,238	58,985	52.5	87.2
29th	72,014	57,102	14,912	57,101	55.8	95.9
30th	66,900	50,015	16,885	50,014	57.2	94.7
31st	74,536	67,883	6,653	67,882	52.3	95.8
33rd	88,507	56,607	31,900	56,606	61.0	121.8
34th	89,905	71,207	18,698	71,206	55.8	108.2
37th	62,623	59,123	3,140	59,122	51.3	95.7
	2,055,611	1,243,609	812,002	1,243,584	63.9	98.0
BY REPUBLICANS:						
6th	98,262	70,151	28,111	70,150	58.3	106.0
10th	103,592	67,695	35,897	67,694	60.5	111.3
11th	98,332	60,308	38,024	60,307	62.0	107.4
12th	75,759	47,731	28,028	47,730	61.3	91.6
13th	84,325	45,513	38,812	45,512	64.9	89.0
14th	93,065	56,149	36,916	56,148	62.4	98.9
20th	114,331	48,069	66,262	48,068	70.4	93.8
24th	115,564	49,610	65,954	49,609	70.0	96.5
28th	156,059	88,791	67,268	88,790	63.7	142.4
32nd	113,063	47,321	65,742	47,320	70.5	105.3
35th	130,687	61,099	69,588	61,098	68.1	114.5
36th	86,519	54,224	32,295	54,223	61.5	101.5
38th	67,986	52,490	15,496	52,489	56.4	91.5
	1,337,544	749,151	588,393	749,138	63.9	103.8

Summary	Democratic Party		Republican Party	
	Number	*Percent*	Number	*Percent*
Congressmen elected	25		13	
Party's percent of total congressmen elected		66.0		34.0
Total votes cast by party	2,804,749		2,581,128	
Party's percent of statewide vote		52.0		48.0
Effective votes	1,243,609		749,151	
Percent effective party votes		34.4		29.5
Excess votes	812,002		588,393	
Percent excess party votes		28.9		22.3
Wasted votes	749,138		1,243,584	
Percent wasted party votes		26.7		48.2

[a] Source, *Congressional Quarterly Weekly Report*, November 16, 1962, p. 2163.

in five of the Democratic districts the winner's majority was over 71 percent, and in two of these it surpassed 80 percent. No Republican, on the other hand, quite achieved a 71 percent majority. In actual fact, then, there were more excess Democratic votes than Republican. This is the kind of result a Republican legislature would have sought to obtain, and it is interesting to note that the Democrats in California could do nothing to reverse the situation.

The best the Democrats could do, therefore, was to waste as many Republican votes as possible. This was achieved by seeing to it that 48.2 percent, almost half, of the Republican ballots were cast in contests where Democrats were elected. Thus, fair-sized minorities of Republicans, averaging about 50,000, were distributed in districts where they would be outvoted. In contrast, only 26.7 percent of the Democratic votes, a little more than a quarter of their total, were wasted by being cast in Republican districts. It is not clear how much of this result can be attributed to the finesse of the Democratic legislature. Californians are unpredictable in their voting habits, and it is difficult to anticipate just where a party's sources of strength will lie. Nevertheless, it is true that of the 25 Democratic victories, 19 were with majorities of 55 percent or higher, a comparatively comfortable margin. Indeed, it would appear that the California Democrats woke up to fewer surprises when the returns were announced than did the New York Republicans.

While the Democrats in California secured a disproportionate number of seats, the percentage they won was not as high as it might conceivably have been.[10] They gained some advantage by locating their candidates in districts of slightly smaller size, but this gain was more than offset by their failure to arrange greater increases in the opposition's excess vote. As it turned out, the Democrats' own excess vote was very high because they won so many of their races with overlarge majorities. Basically, the way the Democrats secured 66 percent of the congressional delegation in 1962 was by wasting Republican strength. In this attempt, they were eminently successful, and the achievement

[10] In the 1954 election, based on districts drawn up by a Republican legislature, the Republicans won 63 percent of California's seats with only 48 percent of the votes. Had their vote risen to 52 percent that year, the Republicans would probably have swept the entire delegation except for one or two Democratic strongholds in central Los Angeles.

should not be minimized in face of the inherent difficulties a Democratic majority encounters when it seeks to distribute its votes to best advantage.

Michigan

The 1962 congressional election in Michigan had much in common with that in New York. In both cases, the districts were Republican creations; and, in both, the Republicans captured a majority of the seats with a minority of votes. But the interesting thing about Michigan compared to New York is that Republicans there did so much better with an even smaller percentage of the statewide vote. As Table 12 shows, with only 48.9 percent of the votes, the Michigan Republicans managed to secure 61 percent of the seats in the congressional delegation.[11] This is real evidence of minority power and its usage deserves examination.

Michigan's districts for the 1962 election were unchanged from those in effect throughout the fifties. This meant that even though substantial population migration had taken place within the state, constituencies were still based on a Census a dozen years out of date. There were good Republican reasons for maintaining the old map. Thirteen of Michigan's 18 districts varied by more than 15 percent of the population norm for the state. While both Republicans and Democrats were located in both large and small districts, Republicans, on the average, were definitely better off. The average Republican seat was 93.9 percent of the norm and the average Democratic seat was 109.5 percent. This difference of 15.6 percent is more than five times the spread in New York and almost three times that in California. Thus, far more than in the other two states, the unequal size of Michigan's districts served to give one party an electoral advantage.

To this was added the dissipation of Democratic strength by concentrating that party's voting support. Four of the seven districts won by the Democrats had majorities of over 69 percent; the largest Repub-

[11] These figures are based on voting in the 18 regular districts. There was, in addition, an election for a single at-large representative, won by a Democrat. The voting in that statewide contest paralleled the aggregate district voting:

Party	At-Large Votes	District Totals
Democrats	1,392,187 (52.1%)	1,322,178 (51.1%)
Republicans	1,280,898 (47.9%)	1,262,992 (48.9%)

TABLE 12. *Voting in 1962 Congressional Elections: Michigan*[a]

(Population norm per district = 434,622)

Districts Won	Winner's Votes			Loser's Wasted Votes	Winner's Majority (Percent)	Percent Population Norm
	Total	Effective	Excess			
BY REPUBLICANS:						
2nd	88,618	63,164	25,454	63,163	58.4	111.2
3rd	77,726	52,688	25,038	52,687	59.5	98.5
4th	72,999	41,637	31,362	41,636	63.7	84.4
5th	109,754	54,053	55,701	54,052	67.0	106.3
6th	112,994	93,854	19,090	93,853	54.6	143.5
8th	77,019	50,373	26,646	50,372	60.5	91.6
9th	65,377	44,591	20,786	44,590	59.5	71.0
10th	62,389	39,601	22,788	39,600	61.2	71.1
11th	45,968	34,839	11,129	34,838	56.9	55.4
12th	41,848	24,251	17,597	24,250	63.3	40.8
18th	149,837	101,483	48,354	101,482	59.6	158.8
	904,479	600,534	303,945	600,523	60.3	93.9
BY DEMOCRATS:						
1st	81,573	7,887	73,686	7,886	89.2	65.2
7th	127,050	98,770	28,280	98,769	56.3	152.9
13th	59,656	24,134	35,522	24,133	71.2	61.7
14th	107,954	67,209	40,745	67,208	61.6	106.3
15th	94,300	19,342	74,958	19,341	83.0	77.5
16th	129,796	57,718	72,078	57,717	69.2	184.8
17th	121,326	83,460	37,866	83,459	59.2	118.0
	721,655	358,520	363,135	358,513	70.0	109.5

Summary	Republican Party		Democratic Party	
	Number	Percent	Number	Percent
Congressmen elected	11		7	
Party's percent of total congressmen elected		61.0		39.0
Total votes cast by party	1,262,992		1,322,178	
Party's percent of statewide vote		48.9		51.1
Effective votes	600,534		358,520	
Percent effective party votes		47.5		27.1
Excess votes	303,945		363,135	
Percent excess party votes		24.1		27.5
Wasted votes	358,513		600,523	
Percent wasted party votes		28.4		45.4

[a] Source, *Congressional Quarterly Weekly Report*, November 16, 1962, pp. 2165–66. Voting in the 18 regular congressional districts. There was also the election of an at-large representative (won by a Democrat), but those figures are not included here.

lican majority was 67 percent, and next highest was 63.7 percent of the votes cast. The average Democratic majority was 70 percent in contrast to the Republicans' 60.3 percent—and this 10 percent difference is a significant figure compared with New York and California. Thus,

27.5 percent of the Democratic votes cast fell in the excess category, in contrast with 24.1 percent of the Republican votes. Since the Democrats won in only seven districts, compared with the Republicans' 11, there were substantially fewer winning contests in which excess votes of the Democrats might have been cast. This inflation of the Democratic excess vote is, of course, related to the inflation of the size of Democratic districts. Thus, even though the Democrats had only a 69.2 percent majority in the 16th District, over 70,000 excess votes were cast there because of its sheer size.

Finally, the Republicans managed to waste Democratic votes by locating them in enemy territory. The average Democratic vote was about 55,000 in Republican districts, and thus 45.4 percent of the Democratic votes could be counted as wasted. This was not as high as Republican wastage in California, but it is a higher figure than the Democratic wastage in New York.

The Michigan Republicans, therefore, used all three of the techniques of gerrymandering. While they had about the same percentage of the popular votes as their colleagues in New York, they secured 10 percent more seats in their congressional delegation. This is because the Michigan legislature, unlike New York's, was willing to add unequal districts to its electoral arsenal.

Summary

An overall comparison may be based on the effective votes of the three gerrymandering parties—the Michigan Republicans, 47.5 percent of its total; the New York Republicans, 44.1 percent; and the California Democrats, 34.4 percent. This is the best single measure of the success of electoral strategy, and on this basis the three parties can be ranked. The Michigan Republicans did as well as they did because they were willing, and able, to use the three available kinds of gerrymander. The New York Republicans were less successful because of their compunctions about creating unequal districts; hence, they could only attempt to increase the Democrats' excess and wasted votes as much as possible. The California Democrats rank last by reason of their ability to make use of only one gerrymandering technique: wasting as many as possible of the opposition's votes. Even had they tried to create large

Republican districts with concentrations of excess Republican votes, it is not clear that the Democrats would have been successful.

It is doubtful that a formula can be created to determine how far each of the gerrymandering methods contributes to a party's effectiveness at the polls. Such an equation would have to solve at least two problems. First, the measurement of excess votes as used here—all those over a one-vote margin of victory—is arbitrary. But any decision about how many votes a party needs for a "comfortable" victory is bound to be controversial. Second, the index of district population employed here is based on the total number of residents rather than the number of voters. Voting turnout varies greatly from district to district, and thus a "large" district may actually have fewer people going to the polls than a "small" one. Furthermore, the population figures are necessarily based on a Census that was two years old by the time the 1962 election was held. Other problems—such as weighting districts so as to allow for their varying total and voting populations—are technical rather than substantive. At all events, the figures used to analyze New York, California, and Michigan should be regarded as illustrative and expository rather than as data suited to a mathematical model.

One final point on this exercise: Allusions to "successful" or "effective" gerrymandering are intended as descriptions, not prescriptions. If bouquets appear to have been bestowed on one party for its cartographical skills, or if another seems to have been chided for its naive self-restraint, these are not moral judgments. A man can be spoken of as a "successful thief," and it is in much the same context that the term "effective gerrymander" is used here. The artistry of a professional safecracker can command admiration even though the ends to which he puts his cunning are deplored.

Motives and Melioration

During the winter and spring of 1961, when congressional redistricting was on the agenda, both houses of the legislature in 42 states were controlled by the same party. And, in 31 of these states, the governor belonged to the party controlling the legislature. It would appear, then, that the way was clear in most states to undermine the opposition

party's electoral fortunes by means of gerrymandering. Is it too cynical to assume that this would be done if possible?

Fair Play in Gerrymandering?

Certainly there are those who talk as if all's fair in love and politics.[12] A Missouri Democrat frankly admitted that no holds are barred:

> Did the Republicans really expect the Democrats to draft and support a redistricting bill favorable to the Republicans? If they did, their political training has been sadly neglected and their political acumen hovers near the zero mark. The Republicans are entitled to the same redistricting feast at the hands of the Democrats that they would serve the Democrats if they were in power. Only that—and nothing more.

And a New York Republican said on the same subject:

> It would be hypocritical for me to deny that the bill may bring about an increased Republican representation in Congress. Of course, that is to be expected of legislation enacted by a legislature which is controlled by the Republicans, because the people of the state voted more Republicans than Democrats into the legislature.

Nor can it be said that gerrymandering lawmakers need have much fear of public disapproval or reprisal. Of all the issues that exercise an electorate, inequitable districting surely is far down on the list. All indications are that relatively few voters know that the problem exists— even citizens living in districts that suffer discrimination. And not many political leaders feel it worth their time and effort to arouse public opinion in this area. Of course, it may be argued that indifference is at least a partial consequence of powerlessness. As Colegrove pointed out almost 20 years ago, there is no point in trying to muster majority sentiment for equal districts if that majority finds itself constitutionally unable to gain control of its state legislature. A majority of the members of the Michigan lower house can be elected by voters in constituencies comprising only 29 percent of the state's population.[13] Hence, it is doubtful if popular resentment against gerrymandering in that state would secure an adequate voice in the capitol.

[12] Both of the following quotations are from Gordon E. Baker, *Rural v. Urban Political Power* (Doubleday, 1955), p. 46.
[13] William J. D. Boyd, *Compendium on Legislative Apportionment* (National Municipal League, 1962), p. iii.

There are those who believe that some restraints are operative. "Extreme gerrymanders, maximizing the predictive ability of the dominant faction," one commentator writes, "are usually prevented . . . by the erring legislators' consciences that provide generally some modicum of shame. . . ."[14] Although the tug of conscience did not appear to be very strong so far as the Republican lawmakers of Michigan were concerned, it may be argued that this is an extreme case. Yet, on the whole, it is difficult to accept the theory that an internalized sense of "fair play" governs actual behavior in this sphere. There are several grounds for such doubts.

First, it is certainly true that a state like New York has for many years refrained from creating congressional districts below 85 percent or above 115 percent of the state population norm. But in New York, as noted earlier, the principle of equal-sized districts was one of the few "rules of the game" to be observed. The dominant party in the legislature then proceeded to show no compunctions about drawing elongated and wandering districts that would increase its electoral strength to the maximum. Conscience was not much in evidence at that stage.

Second, only eight other states (Iowa, Maine, Massachusetts, Minnesota, Nebraska, New Hampshire, North Dakota, and Rhode Island) in addition to New York now have all of their districts within a range of 30 percent of the population norm. Sensibilities about "fair play" may have made a contribution in these nine states. But all of the rest— the vast majority—have drawn up or perpetuated districts outside the 30 percent range. It can only be noted that most states do countenance inequities, which seems to suggest that they are able to bear with their "conscience."

Third, gerrymandering often fails, but not for want of trying. If the California Democrats did not win as many seats as they would have liked, this was mainly because they were unable to relocate their own supporters. Here the restraint was an external one, the product of political ecology, and not a moderating force from within. Certainly, the Democrats in California attempted, insofar as they were able, to concentrate their own adherents in small districts and their opponents in large ones.

---

[14] Alfred de Grazia, "General Theory of Apportionment," *Law and Contemporary Problems, op. cit.,* p. 263.

Finally, there is no denying that when a new party gains a legislative majority in mid-decade it does not redistrict the state's congressional delegation right away but waits until the next Census. This is another of the "rules of the game" in legislative life, for everyone wants to avoid violent seesaws in policy. A party refrains from grasping every immediate opportunity to feather its own nest simply because it would not like to see such opportunism work in the opposite direction when it is out of power. While there is much to be said on both sides of this question, on the whole, it may be suggested that following the rules of the game is less a matter of conscience than it is of long-term self-interest.[15] Indeed, there are many states where the chance of the opposition party's gaining legislative control is extremely slender and, in these instances, permanent gerrymanders can and do occur.

In sum, the politicians quoted earlier are probably closer to the mark than academic commentators who try to find clean motives in what is necessarily a murky enterprise. As a matter of fact, the professionals are quite frank about their roguery; they usually have twinkles in their eyes when they protest that they have done nothing wrong. By the same token, the cries of indignation raised by the opposition are like lines of a familiar play, uttered because everyone expects them. Yet no one believes that the moralistic opposition would not wield as discriminating a drawing pen had they a chance to change the political map.

Compact Constituencies?

The conventional requirements for equitable districting are three in number: that they be compact, contiguous, and roughly equal in population. The last two are easy enough to evaluate. Virtually all districts are comprised of contiguous territory, although there are a few that look like two nations with a thin connecting corridor. (See particularly the 14th and 24th Districts of New York.) So far as population is concerned, it is possible to determine a state norm and to calculate the legitimate range within which a district may deviate from that standard. But New York's experience has demonstrated that significant gerrymandering is possible even when all districts show no more than a 15

[15] For a discussion of "rules of the game" see David Truman, *The Governmental Process* (Knopf, 1951).

percent variation from the norm. This is because the principle of compactness is ignored.

But before a rule on compactness can be enforced (and there is little likelihood that there will be any such rule in the foreseeable future), it must be asked whether what constitutes a "compact" district can ever be anything more than a matter of personal opinion. To be sure, most will agree that a district which meanders across the length of a city or up and down the countryside probably is the result of some Machiavellian motive on the part of the legislature. But not all gerrymandered seats are so obviously distorted. For this reason, it is worth noting that a method has been devised for measuring compactness. There may be a time when courts, if not the Congress, will see fit to use it as one way of deducing the motives behind the map. Its author, Ernest C. Reock, Jr., writes:

> The most compact plane figure is the circle, for here the maximum area is enclosed within a given perimeter. The circle, therefore, can be used as the ideal of compactness, just as the average district population is used as the ideal of population equality. The degree of compactness of any district may be measured by the relationship between the area of the district and the area of the smallest possible circumscribing circle.[16]

No one, of course, expects that a district be circular, or even square. But it is not too difficult to create constituencies that have as much as 75 percent of their territory within a circular "ideal of compactness." Reock took geometric measurements of 90 districts of the 87th Congress and determined the "degree of compactness" for each as follows:

Degree of Compactness	Number of Districts
0- 20.0%	1
20.1- 40.0%	25
40.1- 60.0%	54
60.1- 80.0%	9
80.1-100.0%	1

[16] Ernest C. Reock, Jr., "Measuring Compactness as a Requirement of Legislative Apportionment," *Midwest Journal of Political Science*, Vol. 5 (February 1961), p. 71. And a note is added: "In most cases, the center will be at the midpoint of the longest dimension of the district. In a few instances, the irregularity of the district causes the center to be off-set somewhat from this point. In such cases the center may be found by establishing a triangle formed by the farthest extremities of the district and finding the center of a circle through the points of the triangle."

Unless unusual geographic contours can be shown, the burden of proof would presumably be placed on the mapmakers to explain why a district has a low "degree of compactness." Suspicions of intended gerrymandering, for this sample at least, might arise where the figure fell below 40 percent. For if 64 districts could manage compactness of over 40 percent, then it is proper to ask why the 26 others could not.

This compactness rule, much more than one dealing with equal population, would severely limit legislative manipulation. No longer could the dominant party accumulate a majority for itself by drawing a district that meandered through friendly territory. But this is only one side of the story. Districts can also be too compact—a problem usually far more vexing to the Democratic party than the Republicans. The natural concentration of Democrats has already been discussed in connection with the number of excess votes cast for that party's candidates. A glance at the map of New York City or Detroit will show that the Democratic strongholds in those cities are very compact, and they were purposely made that way by Republican legislatures. If the Democratic representation in Congress is to more closely approximate Democratic votes in cities where such a condition exists, then enforcing a test of compactness may hinder rather than serve that aim.

Related to this is the question of what makes the ideal constituency. One viewpoint is that a district should be relatively homogeneous. Not only would political subdivisions then coincide with natural communities, but groups of citizens would have sufficient power to elect "one of their own kind" to public office. It is in this context that protests arise when "close-knit neighborhoods" are split apart in the process of redistricting. Thus, an editorial complained of the heartless disruption of "historical associations and common interests":

> In modern cities people of similar interests, culture or income tend to live close to one another and to develop close-knit neighborhoods. Over the years these form harmonious and durable ties with surrounding neighborhoods of somewhat different cultural backgrounds. The people in such groups of neighborhoods have every right to expect that the state, in readjusting Congressional and legislative districts, will take cognizance of their historical associations and common interests so that any change will entail minimum disruption of their traditional political pattern.[17]

[17] *New York Times*, Jan. 24, 1962.

This is a rather romantic conception of today's large city. But even if it were a valid depiction, it should not be assumed that the urban voter is served best by merging cultural neighborhood boundaries with those of the constituency. To be sure, some voters receive a certain psychic gratification from having a congressman of Irish, Italian, Polish, Jewish, or Negro background. On the other hand, districts where this occurs usually cast excessively large majorities for one party. For example, the residents of Harlem, despite possibly "similar interests, culture, or income," do not make the most of their political power by being crowded into a single district and electing a Negro representative by a majority that runs to 70 percent and often higher. (Harlem's 18th District, it should be added, is a model of compactness considering the shape of Manhattan Island.) Using their votes to far better advantage are the citizens of upstate New York, where rural areas and small towns are merged in a single district with medium-sized cities. All in all, the compact and homogeneous constituency has severe drawbacks for those who live in it. Certainly, it is not clear that setting a standard of compactness would solve more gerrymandering problems than it would create, or at least perpetuate.

There are several reasons for believing that current concern should focus on more equal population for congressional districts. It is quite plain, first of all, that geometric tests for compactness are not going to be established or enforced for some time to come. While the techniques of gerrymandering can give disproportionate representation to a party, it is also true that this advantage is substantially lessened if the gerrymandering party must work within the framework of roughly equal districts. Moreover, it is hard to conceive of "neutral" districts, no matter who draws them up or whatever purity of motive may inform the enterprise. Urban Democrats, for example, may claim that they are penalized by even purportedly neutral districts and would, therefore, ask for some benevolent gerrymandering to bring them up to a parity with the more strategically located Republicans. The Republicans may reply that what the Democratic party loses in northern cities it makes up in the South. Support for this assertion can be found in the figures at the opening of this chapter showing that if the Congress is taken as a whole the Democrats get more representatives for fewer votes. And to all this the liberal will glumly add that the conservatives seem to win either way. There is no simple solution.

These questions involving partisan and ideological advantage are both interesting and important, and should not be skirted simply because they touch on controversial points. At the same time, there is some obligation to concentrate attention where change is most likely to occur. Gerrymandering will doubtless persist, for little can be done to implant the seeds of "fair play" in soil that is not hospitable; and it is clear that plans—no matter how ingenious—for measuring the contours of districts will not be given much legislative attention. At this stage then, a judicial hearing is being given to the proposition that all legislative districts should embrace equal numbers of citizens. If there is to be reform at all, this is where it is likely to be.

4

Unequal Representation: Characteristics and Consequences

GERRYMANDERS ADD WEIGHT to some citizens' votes, and the changing fortunes of the parties in successive elections can lead to disproportionate representation. However, these gains and losses vary from state to state and year to year, and cannot easily be measured. What can be gauged are inequities arising from the fact that congressional districts are unequal in size. A voter living in a small, and hence overrepresented, district casts a weightier ballot than a citizen residing in one that is large, and consequently underrepresented. Variations in the value of a vote that stem from disparities in the size of districts are easily ascertained by comparing the number of individuals assigned to different congressional seats.

Most of this chapter will be occupied with asking which Americans benefit and which suffer discrimination because of the unequal size of districts. These benefits and discriminations are not distributed at random, and discovering the characteristics of overrepresented and underrepresented seats is a worthwhile pursuit.

The points of demarcation to be used here are widely accepted. The American Political Science Association has defined an "equitable" district as one within a 30 percent spread, ranging from 85 percent to 115 percent of the state norm.[1] The norm, it will be recalled, is the population that all districts of a state would have if the number of seats in the

[1] This standard was set by a committee of the American Political Science Association in 1951, and it has been accepted as the basis for most legislative proposals. See "The Reapportionment of Congress," *American Political Science Review*, Vol. 45 (March 1951), pp. 154-55.

congressional delegation were divided into the state's total population. This method would produce the following results, as of 1960, for New York, California, and Michigan (based on Tables 10, 11, and 12 in Chapter 3).

State	1960 State Norm	Overrepresented Districts (Under 85%)	Equitable Districts (85% to 115%)	Underrepresented Districts (Over 115%)
New York	409,324	0	41	0
California	413,611	3	29	6
Michigan	434,622	8	5	5

Congressional Districts in the 1950's

The focus here is primarily historical. The decade of the 1950's is studied because data and experience for that period have been accumulated and it is possible to draw some generalizations about the characteristics of large and small districts. Moreover, it is probable that the 1960's will not differ too greatly in these respects from the immediately preceding years.

If the size of districts is to be computed, then a particular point in time must be established. The distribution of overrepresented, equitable, and underrepresented seats for New York, California, and Michigan just cited was correct for the 1960 Census year. But even now those figures are out of date. For the rate of growth in some districts outdistances that of the state as a whole, and other districts lag behind. A seat classed as equitable at the time of the Census may well be over-populated or underpopulated several years later. To take account of intrastate migrations during the 1950's, therefore, the size of each district was set at its estimated population at mid-decade. This estimate of the 1955 size is simply the average of the 1950 and 1960 Census counts for every district.[2] In addition, the base figure to be employed will be 426 congressional districts rather than the full membership of 435 in

[2] The 1950 and 1960 figures on district populations are in U. S. Bureau of the Census, *Congressional District Data Book, Districts of the 87th Congress,* a supplement to *Statistical Abstract of the United States* (1961). It goes without saying that the rate of growth in most districts was not linear. However, only a 10-year period is being dealt with here and a simple average ought not to do too much violence to the facts.

the House of Representatives. The nine seats set to one side were not "districts" in the sense that they embraced only a portion of a state's population. Four of the nine were the at-large seats apportioned to states receiving a single congressman (Delaware, Nevada, Vermont, Wyoming). Four others were from two states, each of which had two representatives and elected both of them on an at-large basis (New Mexico and North Dakota). The ninth was an at-large seat in a state that was otherwise divided into regular districts (Connecticut).[3] These districts were eliminated from consideration because all of them were "equitable" by definition rather than design. When a congressional seat covers an entire state then every citizen has a vote of equal value just as he does for senator or governor.[4]

In the middle of the 1950's, 229 districts were within the equitable range based on the population norm, and 197 were outside. Of the latter number, 106 were overrepresented, and 91 were underrepresented.

Overrepresented (below 85% of the norm)	106	25%
Equitable (85% to 115% of the norm)	229	54%
Underrepresented (over 115% of the norm)	91	21%
	426	100%

In 1955, then, over half of these districts could be considered as equitable in size. But this was not to last for long. By the end of the decade, only 43 percent of the seats remained within the equitable range. Also, in 1955, 15 more districts were overrepresented than underrepresented; and, by 1960, this difference amounted to 25. The reason for this disproportion is that American migration has not been

[3] Texas and Washington each had one at-large seat, in addition to their regular districts, for the 1952, 1954, and 1956 elections. Both states redistricted in time for the 1958 and 1960 elections, and these new districts were used in the computations. Alaska elected its first congressman in 1958, raising the House membership to 436; and Hawaii did the same in 1960, raising it to 437. However, as both of these were single-seat states they were excluded from the analysis.

[4] The problem of whether at-large districts should be considered equitable is a difficult one to answer. While all citizens have an equal "share" in their state's at-large congressman, it is so small a share that its value as a form of representation is open to question. And the existence of an at-large seat inevitably enlarges the size of the regular districts. Moreover, the creation of at-large seats by states gaining congressmen is quite frankly an attempt on the part of the dominant party to continue existing population inequities among regular districts and, if possible, to promote the political career of one of its own members by elevating him to statewide prominence.

symmetrical. The exodus has been from widely scattered districts, while a much smaller group of districts has been receiving the influx. One suburban constituency, for example, that doubles in size during a decade will recruit its entrants from numerous urban and rural districts throughout the nation.

District Characteristics

As a basis for judging district characteristics, five elements have been selected which cover political, economic, and social attributes of the people residing in the various congressional districts. These are:

1. Party Competition. Does one type of district give more evidence of two-party competition than the others?

2. Electoral Participation. Is there higher voter turnout in one kind of district than another?

3. Standard of Living. Is the material condition of life superior in one sort of district compared with the others?

4. Party Support. Are Democrats or Republicans more apt to be found in a certain kind of district?

5. Population Composition. Is one class of district more likely to embrace rural, urban, or some other kind of population?

In all of these cases, the distribution of characteristics among the overrepresented, the equitable, and the underrepresented districts are compared with their distribution among the total number of congressional seats. The total, of course, should not be regarded as a norm or a fair arrangement. After all, almost half of all districts are overrepresented or underrepresented. The aggregate distribution is simply provided in each table for comparative, rather than normative, purposes.

Party Competition

Judging from Table 13, the safer a district, the more likely it is to be overrepresented; as it becomes more competitive, the district is likely to move toward underrepresentation. The uncontested districts, of course, are primarily in the South. But even if they are left out of consideration, it is clear that more equitable and underrepresented seats

TABLE 13. *Size and Party Competition: 426 Congressional Districts*[a]

(In percentages)

Size by Population Norm	Uncontested 95 Districts	Safe 160 Districts	Fighting 70 Districts	Doubtful 101 Districts	Total 426 Districts
Overrepresented (under 85%)	33	25	23	19	25
Equitable (85–115%)	50	53	56	56	54
Underrepresented (over 115%)	17	22	21	25	21

[a] Sources, *Complete Returns of the 1960 Election*, Special Report of Congressional Quarterly Service, March 10, 1961; and *Congressional Quarterly Almanac, 85th Cong. 2 sess.*, Congressional Quarterly Service, Vol. 14 (1958). Party competition based on percentage of votes that winner received in 1958 congressional election as follows: uncontested, no major-party opposition; safe, 60–99.9 percent; fighting, 55–59.9 percent; and doubtful, less than 55 percent.

are classed as "doubtful." This correlation should not be surprising. A small district stands a better chance of being homogeneous in character and, therefore, tending to support a single party. Larger districts, with the exception of some of the big urban districts, usually encompass a diverse population, giving rise to party competition. If competition is regarded as an end worth pursuing, then the equalization of district size would be a step in that direction. Despite gerrymandering techniques, it becomes more difficult to ensure the safety of a district as its population approximates the state norm. The earlier comparison of gerrymandering efforts by New York and Michigan Republicans showed that the New York party's scope for manipulation was limited by the fact that all districts had to be within the equitable range.

If small size makes for safety, safe congressmen are also successful in keeping their districts small. Perhaps the most striking instance of this in the 1950's was the late Sam Rayburn's freedom from electoral worries. His friends in the Texas legislature steadfastly kept his district one of the smallest in the nation: 57 percent of the state norm in 1955. Right next door was the district containing Dallas which, at 195 percent of the norm, had parts which could easily have been transferred to Rayburn's district. But the Dallas district contained Republican voters and their intrusion might have discomfited the Speaker of the House.

Doubtful districts, on the other hand, have a high turnover in incumbents, and such representatives are not likely to have the time or the resources with which to build up legislative favor. The residents of such districts, therefore, are likely to suffer from underrepresentation, and one reason they are shown so little sympathy at the state capitol is that they are so inconstant in their partisan loyalties. Voters showing independence of mind are not always the object of courtship. On the contrary, they are frequently penalized for their lack of party loyalty at the polls.

Electoral Participation

The 426 districts covered in Table 14 were ranked in order of the percentage of their adult residents turning out to vote in the 1958 congressional elections. The districts were then divided into thirds, the first having the highest incidence of electoral participation and the third the lowest. The highest third contained more overrepresented districts and fewer underrepresented ones than the total distribution for the Congress. The middle third, on the other hand, had the opposite disproportion, with more large districts and fewer small ones. And the lowest third comes closest to approximating the general congressional picture.

It may safely be assumed that most of the districts in the lowest third are in the South, where the turnout of voters is very small. But if the bottom third is eliminated from consideration, what emerges is that small districts have higher voting participation than do large ones. The

TABLE 14. *Size and Electoral Participation: 426 Congressional Districts*[a]

(In percentages)

Size by Population Norm	Highest Third 142 Districts	Middle Third 143 Districts	Lowest Third 141 Districts	Total 426 Districts
Overrepresented (under 85%)	33	13	29	25
Equitable (85–115%)	53	58	50	54
Underrepresented (over 115%)	14	29	22	21

[a] Source, U. S. Bureau of the Census, *Congressional District Data Book, Districts of the 87th Congress*, a supplement to *Statistical Abstract of the United States* (1961). Electoral participation is based on the percent of adult residents who voted in the 1958 congressional election and on the 1960 Census, as follows: highest third, 53.7–87.4 percent; middle third, 42.2–53.6 percent; and lowest third, 2.5–42.1 percent.

chief reason for this is that rural districts in the North, both Republican and Democratic, have high turnouts and are also overrepresented. But this is by no means a total explanation, and it is partially offset by the fact that underrepresented suburban seats also have high voting rates. All in all, the factors making for participation are not easily correlated with the size of a district. It might be speculated that underrepresented citizens do not bother to vote because they feel that their voice in Congress is muted. But it is very doubtful that many voters stay at home for so sophisticated a reason as that.

Standard of Living

Districts were also ranked in Table 15, in an order reflecting their material prosperity.[5] Those in the poorest third stand better than a three-to-one chance of being overrepresented as opposed to underrepresented; and those in the most prosperous third are more than twice as likely to be underrepresented as overrepresented. The chief cause of this maldistribution is that over 70 percent of the rural districts are in the bottom third. By the same token, virtually all the suburban constituencies are in the wealthiest third. These figures on standard of living do suggest one point which will be subsequently elaborated. Citizens who have failed to prosper in economic terms, and this is the case for most of those who inhabit rural America, often seek to redress this handicap by perpetuating unequal political representation for themselves. Not all poor Americans, to be sure, are in a position to acquire or to maintain such disproportionate power. But state legislatures are sympathetic to country voters and they pass on to them a greater voice

[5] While there is a good deal of Census information on income and material possessions (extending even to home freezers and air conditioning units), none of it is broken down by congressional districts. The only information in the *Congressional District Data Book, op. cit.*, deals with the condition of housing. Census enumerators described every dwelling as either "sound" or "deteriorating" or "dilapidated." Thus, the districts were arranged in order of the percentage of dwellings they had in the "sound" category.

So far as can be determined there was no geographic bias in the decision as to whether a dwelling was in good condition. That is, both urban tenements and rural shanties stood the same chances of being classified as unsound. A poor city district (New York's 16th, which covered Harlem) had about the same proportion of "deteriorating" or "dilapidated" dwellings as a poor rural district (Mississippi's 1st District).

TABLE 15. *Size and Standard of Living: 426 Congressional Districts*[a]

(In percentages)

Size by Population Norm	Highest Third 142 Districts	Middle Third 141 Districts	Lowest Third 143 Districts	Total 426 Districts
Overrepresented (under 85%)	14	22	38	25
Equitable (85–115%)	52	59	50	54
Underrepresented (over 115%)	34	29	11	21

[a] Source, *Congressional District Data Book, op. cit.* Standard of living based on 1960 Census of Housing, in order of the percentage of dwellings in sound condition as following: highest third, 84.6–97.5 percent; middle third, 76.2–84.5 percent; and lowest third, 47.7–76.1 percent.

in Congress. Not the least rationalization for this is the claim that the countryside "needs" added political weight to counteract the economic power of the cities. If wealthier individuals tend to be underrepresented in Congress, the argument goes, they are not without influence in other circles where decisions are made.

Party Support

The three congressional elections of 1956, 1958, and 1960 were used in Table 16 as a measure of a district's identification with one party or the other. During this period, only 61 of the 426 districts shifted allegiance one or more times. The rest remained constant, even if the dominant party's majority did on occasion become rather tenuous. In fact, the great majority of congressional seats do not change from one party to another over a long period of years.

Taken as a whole, Republican districts reflected the overall congressional distribution. While there may be concern about disproportionate Republican power in the legislatures of many northern states, that control apparently has not helped Republican congressmen to secure an undue share of small constituencies in such states. Northern Democratic representatives, on the other hand, had appreciably less than the Republican proportion of underrepresented seats. The chief reason is that urban districts are unlikely to be underrepresented because they have been losing, rather than gaining, population over the decade. Not a few seats in Chicago, Philadelphia, and Detroit were underrepresented in 1950, but were in the equitable range by 1955. And by 1960 several had, because of further population losses, even reached the overrepresented category. In these terms, the northern Democrats do comparatively well, until time for the next reapportionment—when the cycle begins all over again. There were fewer southern Democratic seats in the equitable range, and a very large number were overrepresented. This means that the southern states created a great many small constituencies, most of them rural, and then proceeded to concentrate much of the remaining population in a handful of particularly large urban seats. Thus, while only 21 percent of the southern Democratic districts were classed as underrepresented, this percentage does not indicate the extent of crowding in some of them. In 1955, for example, Alabama's 9th District (Birmingham) stood at 169 percent of the state norm in terms of population; Tennessee's 9th District (Memphis) was at 146 percent; and Georgia's 5th District (Atlanta) was as high as 195 percent. Even larger was Texas' 5th District (Dallas) which elected a Republican congressman and, hence, was not counted in this group. Nevertheless, the 5th District's huge size—199.5 percent of the norm—permitted absorption of enough Texans so that rural Democrats elsewhere in the state could have the pleasure of being overrepresented.

TABLE 16. *Size and Party Support: 426 Congressional Districts*[a]

(In percentages)

Size by Population Norm	Constant			Changing 61 Districts	Total 426 Districts
	Northern Democratic 125 Districts	Southern Democratic 99 Districts	Republican 141 Districts		
Overrepresented (under 85%)	25	32	22	20	25
Equitable (85–115%)	60	47	55	50	54
Underrepresented (over 115%)	15	21	23	30	21

[a] Source, *Congressional District Data Book, op. cit.* Party support based on 1956, 1958, and 1960 congressional elections. Districts are classed according to whether they elected a congressman from the same party in all three elections. Southern states are the eleven formerly belonging to the Confederacy. Seven southern Republican districts were classified as Republican.

When the northern and southern segments of the Democratic party
are combined, it is clear that the Democrats fare better than the Republicans in terms of representation. The real losers, however, are the
voters living in changing districts. These seats are mainly in the "doubtful" category discussed earlier, and it has been shown why they are so
prone to underrepresentation.

Population Composition

It is no easy task to classify congressional districts by the kind of
people who live in them. To be sure, there are many that fit easily into
the "urban" or "rural" categories. However, the average constituency
embraces about 400,000 residents, spreading over an extensive area and
including a mixed population. Thus, a district may contain a medium-
sized city at its center, a growing suburban fringe, and then a substantial stretch of countryside at its edges. Quite clearly such a district
can be classified in more than one way. The simplest classification
scheme has been devised by the Bureau of the Census. It defines as
"urban" any community with a population of 2,500 or more. Under this
definition, there were no less than 5,445 cities in the United States in
1960, and 69.9 percent of all Americans were classed as "urban population." Consequently, the Census Bureau calls a congressional seat an
"urban" district if a majority of its inhabitants live in towns with more
than 2,500 residents. Using this method, the Bureau concluded that
there were 300 "urban" districts and 137 "rural" districts.[6]

The obvious difficulty with this method is that a town of 2,500 is
much too small to be called "urban." Indeed, cities of 10 or even 20
times that size are usually more rural than urban in their social characteristics and political orientation. The Census Bureau, it should be
added, is not far from the mark in saying that there are 137 districts
predominantly rural in population composition. However, its "urban"
category is too large.

A more sophisticated system of classification has been devised by
the *Congressional Quarterly,* based on the Census Bureau's identification of 213 "urbanized areas" in the country.[7] Each of these areas con-

[6] Bureau of the Census, Release CB62-23, February 24, 1962.
[7] *Congressional Quarterly Weekly Report,* February 2, 1962, pp. 153-69.

tains at least one central city with a population of over 50,000. The largest of these is the New York-Northeastern area (with 1960 population of 14,114,927) and the smallest is Tyler, Texas (51,739). Urban districts were defined by the *Congressional Quarterly* as those having the greater part of their population living in the central city that formed the heart of the urbanized area. In addition, certain congressional districts were classified as "suburban" if the greater portion of their inhabitants resided in what the Census Bureau defined as the "fringe" of the urbanized area. Finally, all districts having the greater part of their population outside the 213 urbanized areas were classed as rural. The resulting *Congressional Quarterly* breakdown was: 126 urban districts, 60 suburban districts, and 250 rural districts.

Whereas the Census Bureau went too far in one direction, exaggerating the number of "urban" districts, *Congressional Quarterly* errs in the other direction in concluding that there are 250 districts that may properly be called "rural." A second difficulty is that the *Congressional Quarterly* defined a district as urban or suburban or rural on the basis of which type of population was most prevalent. Thus, the 5th District of Michigan was called "urban" even though its population was only 38.4 percent urban, with the remainder being 25.3 percent suburban and 36.3 percent rural. While there was more urban population in this district than either of the other two types, it is clear that Grand Rapids does not dominate or typify the constituency. Indeed, there are quite mixed populations in a large proportion of the *Congressional Quarterly's* "rural" districts.

Nevertheless, the *Congressional Quarterly* method is basically sound, and the classification scheme employed here is a modification of it. As most congressional districts contain mixtures of urban, suburban, and rural population, a seat will be classed according to the proportion of its inhabitants living in each type of area. A fourth category, to be called "mid-urban," has been devised to characterize districts that are not preponderantly urban or suburban or rural. The proportions used are as follows:

URBAN—An urban district is one with 60 percent or more of its inhabitants living in the central city of one of the 213 urbanized areas in the country. In 1955, a typical district contained slightly less than 400,000 people. Therefore, a district that was at least 60 percent urban would lie inside or embrace a city of 250,000 or more. There can, of course, be no objective judgment as to when a medium-sized town turns into a large city. What can be said at this point is that for purposes of this study, when a city reaches 250,000, it apparently begins to have the attributes and interests of a metropolitan center. The problems and attitudes of the residents of Tyler, Texas, and Chicago, Illinois, are quite different even though both are classed as urbanized areas. But if the minimum size is raised to about 250,000, then the smallest city is more like Toledo, Ohio, which does have much in common with Chicago.[8]

SUBURBAN—A suburban district is here classified as one having 50 percent or more of its residents living on the fringes of an urbanized area. Virtually every city over 20,000 in America today has its "suburbs." But these are usually very small and they blend with open country quite soon. Moreover, since a typical congressional district contains 400,000 people, very few suburbs are large enough to take up a whole district. If suburban population is less than half of a district's total population then it is improbable that a uniquely suburban outlook will permeate the entire constituency. Therefore, it is preferable to reserve this designation for districts where at least half the residents are suburbanites. If this is done, then suburban districts mainly will be found surrounding the 10 largest cities of the United States. Suburbs of smaller cities are themselves too small to cover more than a fraction of a district.

RURAL—Next, a rural district is classified as one with 90 percent or more of its population occupying territory outside the 213 urbanized areas. The percentage has been set this high simply to ensure that rural districts will have no cities of over 50,000 within their boundaries, or at most only a very small part of such a city or its fringe area. Even so, this does not mean that rural districts will be primarily agricultural. They can, and do, contain towns of 40,000 or so; and many have industry, often drawing their labor force from those who live on farms but drive

---

[8] A few large cities were placed in such large districts that even though they were over 250,000 their residents did not account for 60 percent or more of a single congressional district. This was the case with Atlanta, Birmingham, and Oklahoma City. Despite their size, they still could not be said to dominate the districts of which they were a part.

appreciable distances to work in a factory.[9] There is no harm in calling these districts "rural" so long as the term is understood in its contemporary context.

MID-URBAN—All remaining districts, and they form the largest single group, are here referred to as "mid-urban." This is not simply a residual category, but rather one that seeks to describe districts that are not really urban, suburban, or rural. The typical district contains approximately 400,000 people and this may be a heterogeneous population in terms of geographic composition. Put another way, only a fraction of all congressional districts are composed of "pure" urban or suburban or rural territory. At the same time, the districts to be called mid-urban follow a fairly standard pattern. They include all or part of a medium-sized city, ranging in population from 50,000 to 250,000. While the major city or cities in the district will be surrounded by a suburban fringe, this city-suburb combination is not large enough to dominate the entire constituency. By the same token, the outlying rural area also lacks the strength to impose its way of thinking on the whole district.

There is evidence that the outlook and behavior of congressmen from mid-urban seats differ from those of men representing districts that are primarily urban or rural. In addition, there is a higher incidence of doubtful districts and meaningful two-party competition than in the other categories. Also mid-urban seats differ from the others in terms of equality in congressional representation (see Table 17). In sum, it would be a mistake to try to force mid-urban districts into an urban-suburban-rural trichotomy. They have an existence of their own and that status should be recognized. Thus a fourfold classification, modifying the *Congressional Quarterly* method, yields the following division: 91 urban districts, 52 suburban, 181 mid-urban, and 102 rural.

None of these groups offers a close approximation of the general distribution of congressional seats, as Table 17 reveals. The urban districts

[9] The 36th District of New York, containing Cornell University, was classified by the *Congressional Quarterly* as 100 percent rural. This was proper as the district contained no "urbanized area" nor did it impinge upon one. Nevertheless, it had within its borders towns of 35,249 (Auburn) and 28,799 (Ithaca) so it was not entirely bucolic. Furthermore, the district had 87,300 male residents between the ages of 21 and 65, yet only 10,500 were employed in farming occupations. This means that 88 percent of the employment-age men in a 100 percent rural district were earning their livings elsewhere than on the land. This pattern is not untypical for so-called rural America.

were actually better represented than is commonly believed. The reason for this, pointed out earlier in the discussion of northern Democratic seats, is that large cities have not been gaining in population and thus have been able to preserve equitable representation for themselves.

TABLE 17. *Size and Population Composition: 426 Congressional Districts*[a]

(In percentages)

Size by Population Norm	Urban 91 Districts	Suburban 52 Districts	Mid-Urban 181 Districts	Rural 102 Districts	Total 426 Districts
Overrepresented (under 85%)	20	13	17	49	25
Equitable (85–115%)	61	35	60	45	54
Underrepresented (over 115%)	19	52	23	6	21

[a] Source, *Congressional Quarterly Weekly Report*, February 2, 1962. Population composition based on 1960 Census of urbanized areas, with districts classified as follows: urban, 60 percent or more urban population; suburban, 50 percent or more urban-fringe population; rural, 90 percent or more nonurban population; and mid-urban, all other districts.

The opposing tendency holds in the case of suburban voters, a majority of whom were underrepresented. As the population of a suburban district skyrockets year by year, so each suburban vote is progressively devalued as the decade moves forward. Yet, even when the time for redistricting arrives, rural-dominated state legislatures often perpetuate the overlarge districts which include the suburbs. And this can be true even if those suburbs elect congressmen wearing the same party label as that worn by the majority in the legislature. For within a single party in various states there are deep-seated tensions between the rural and suburban factions. For these reasons, suburban voters have experienced the greatest losses in congressional representation.

Table 17, on the other hand, shows that almost half of the rural districts were overrepresented. This is partly because rural areas, like large cities, lost population during the decade. But much more important is the fact that state legislatures deliberately gave full congressional representation to combinations of rural counties that fell below the population norm. Indeed, most of the losses suffered by suburban voters appear to have redounded to the favor of their country cousins.

The mid-urban districts fared worse than the strictly urban ones. They had a greater share of underrepresented seats and a smaller share of overrepresented seats than either the urban districts or the entire Congress. One cause is that mid-urban areas were, on balance, growing in population. Another is that they contained a large proportion of doubtful seats, which are often targets of discrimination. What emerges is that mid-urban districts rank third among the four groups in terms of the value of each resident's vote and the equitable representation of the population.

If party support and population composition of districts are cross-tabulated, a more precise idea can be had of who gained and who lost representation as a result of the unequal size of constituencies. One way to make such a comparison is to contrast the actual distribution of seats with a weighted distribution based on population. The weighted distribution was arrived at by multiplying the districts in each of the 16 categories by their number of inhabitants. Thus, each district was given a weight proportionate to its population. The weighted distribution used in Table 18 therefore shows how the Congress might have been constituted if each of the categories had representatives corresponding to their population.

The actual distributions themselves are of some intrinsic interest in showing the sources of strength of each of the party groups. Thus, the northern wing of the Democratic party relies less heavily on urban support than is often believed, and the greatest concentration of both Republican and southern Democratic strength is in mid-urban districts. Moreover, the Republicans do not dominate the rural and suburban seats to the extent commonly thought. While it is tempting to enter into further speculation and analysis in this area, the question at issue is how far the actual distribution of seats gave added representation to some groups of districts and diminished representation to others.

So far as party was concerned, the Democrats had five more seats than they would have had if district population governed the distribution of districts. The Republicans had one less seat than they theoretically deserved. And the chief losers were the residents of the changing districts, which had four fewer seats than they deserved—a particularly severe loss considering that there were only 61 districts in that category.

TABLE 18. *Actual and Weighted Distribution of Congressional Seats: Party Support and Population Composition in 426 Districts*

Party and Composition	Distribution		Difference	Composition and Party	Distribution		Difference
	Actual	Weighted			Actual	Weighted	
NORTHERN DEMOCRATIC:				URBAN:			
Urban	54	52	+2	Northern Democratic	54	52	+2
Suburban	15	17	−2	Southern Democratic	9	12	−3
Mid-urban	32	33	−1	Republican	18	17	+1
Rural	24	20	+4	Changing	10	10	0
Total	125	122	+3	Total	91	91	0
SOUTHERN DEMOCRATIC:				SUBURBAN:			
Urban	9	12	−3	Northern Democratic	15	17	−2
Suburban	2	2	0	Southern Democratic	2	2	0
Mid-urban	50	50	0	Republican	27	32	−5
Rural	38	33	+5	Changing	8	11	−3
Total	99	97	+2	Total	52	62	−10
REPUBLICAN:				MID-URBAN:			
Urban	18	17	+1	Northern Democratic	32	33	−1
Suburban	27	32	−5	Southern Democratic	50	50	0
Mid-urban	70	72	−2	Republican	70	72	−2
Rural	26	21	+5	Changing	29	32	−3
Total	141	142	−1	Total	181	187	−6
CHANGING:				RURAL:			
Urban	10	10	0	Northern Democratic	24	20	+4
Suburban	8	11	−3	Southern Democratic	38	33	+5
Mid-urban	29	32	−3	Republican	26	21	+5
Rural	14	12	+2	Changing	14	12	+2
Total	61	65	−4	Total	102	86	+16

With regard to population composition, it is clear that the 16-seat gain for rural districts was paid for by the deprivations of 10 seats and 6 seats experienced respectively by suburban and mid-urban groups. The actual and weighted distributions of population composition for total urban seats were identical, reinforcing the point that of all the categories the large cities have been treated most equitably.

But these general conclusions conceal some interesting variations within the major groups. Thus, if the southern Democratic group had only two more seats than its number of inhabitants would warrant, this is because three of its overrepresented rural districts and its three underrepresented urban districts canceled each other out. The same process took place within the Republican camp, where large suburban seats were offset by small rural ones. In both cases, therefore, the rural districts gain extra seats primarily because urban or suburban districts of their own party are the objects of discrimination. In sum then, there is a good deal of intraparty parasitism, especially in states where rural areas have retained a significant measure of power.

Except for the urban districts, the categories based on population composition are fairly consistent in either gaining or losing seats. Within the urban group, the nine southern Democratic districts were so heavily underrepresented as to cancel the slight overrepresentation of the 72 Republican and northern Democratic seats. Perhaps most striking is the fact that half of the six-seat handicap of the mid-urban group came from the severe underrepresentation of the 29 changing districts in that category. In percentage terms, the changing districts fared as badly as the suburban seats on some occasions, and somewhat worse on others. Finally, it should be noted that northern Democratic districts made their contribution to rural overrepresentation, although not to the same degree as Republican and southern Democratic seats.

The problem of rural overrepresentation, therefore, is very real. Districts with predominantly rural population had 102 congressmen, whereas their actual numbers would have entitled them to only 86. This was a net gain of 16 seats. Suburban underrepresentation is more serious than that suffered by mid-urban citizens simply because there are far fewer suburban seats and their 10-seat loss is an extremely heavy one. The other strongly underrepresented group consists of the urban Democrats in the South, a beleaguered minority continually victimized by the region's widespread mistrust of metropolitan life.

Consequences for Policy

In his testimony before a House of Representatives subcommittee considering the problem of districting, Democratic Congressman Ken Hechler of West Virginia raised an intriguing question:

> I am sure you can all recall crucial rollcall votes, over the past few Congresses, that were decided by as few as 10 votes. Did the winning side on those close votes actually represent a majority of the people? It is quite possible they did not.[10]

[10] In *Standards for Congressional Districts (Apportionment)*, Hearings before Subcommittee No. 2 of the House Committee on the Judiciary, 86th Cong. 1st sess. (1959), p. 32.

This is an interesting speculation and it deserves to be tested. Certainly the 87th Congress witnessed some very close roll calls. Had districts been of equal size would the outcomes of close roll calls have been different?

One way to approach this question is to assume that the 87th Congress had the same individuals as representatives, but that each member's roll-call vote was weighted so as to reflect the population of his district. This is, of course, an artificial assumption, for if districts were of equal size then it is highly probable that different sorts of congressmen would be elected. If a small rural district were increased in size and had added to it a leaven of urban population, then either the incumbent would be replaced or he would alter his voting habits so as to accommodate the new interests in his constituency. While this is true, and is one of the motive forces behind the pressure for more equal districts, it is nevertheless necessary to work with the members of the House of Representatives who actually sat in the 87th Congress. For it is not possible to talk about congressmen who have not yet been elected.

There are two methods of weighting that may be used. The first is to weight each representative's vote on a bill by the population of his district. Thus, if he comes from a small district his vote will be proportionately smaller than that of a colleague from a district, say, double the size.[11] An alternative method grows out of the realization that population as an index has certain inadequacies. In many districts, only a small proportion of the eligible adults vote; for example, it is not clear that the largely disenfranchised Negro population of some districts in the South is being represented by their congressmen in more than name. And there is the recurrent problem of the extent to which a representative speaks for those who voted for his opponent in the previous election. For these reasons, it has been proposed that roll-call votes be weighted, not by the district's population, but rather by the number of votes the congressman received at the polls.[12] This method not only gives greater weights to congressmen from larger districts, but it also

[11] This plan has been suggested by Ruth Silva, and was included in her staff report to the New York Temporary Commission on Revision and Simplification of the Constitution in April 1960. It is summarized in a press release from Station WMCA, New York City, May 10, 1962, p. 7.

[12] This proposal originated with Robert H. Engle. See his "Weighting Legislators' Votes to Equalize Representation," *Western Political Quarterly*, Vol. 12 (June 1959), pp. 442-48.

increases the influence of those receiving excessively high majorities due to gerrymandering.

Four roll-call votes of the 87th Congress[13] have been weighted by both of these methods, with the results shown in Table 19. All four were roll calls on proposals having vigorous Administration support, and three of the four were defeated:

1. Urban Affairs. House Resolution 530, which was carried by a 271 to 156 vote on February 21, 1962, disapproved the reorganization plan that would have created a Department of Urban Affairs at cabinet level.

2. Education. HR 8890, which was defeated by a 251 to 179 vote on August 30, 1961, was the Emergency Educational Aid bill that was a key part of President Kennedy's domestic program.

3. Agriculture. HR 11222, which was defeated by 222 to 212 on the passage of a motion to recommit on June 21, 1962, was the annual Food and Agriculture bill offered by the Administration.

4. Rules Committee. House Resolution 127, which passed by a margin of 219 to 214 on January 31, 1961, added three members to the Rules Committee.

Congressman Hechler's speculation suggests that at least one of the three defeats—Agriculture—might have been turned into victory had districts been of equal size, and that the single razor-edge victory—Rules—might have been a more substantial one. Yet, when the roll-call votes are weighted, a quite different picture emerges. In all four cases, with representatives' votes weighted by their districts' populations, the Administration side would have received fewer votes. It would have lost the urban affairs, education, and agriculture bills by greater margins than it actually did; and, most startling, the resolution enlarging the Rules Committee would have been defeated. With weighting by popular votes, the outcomes would have been more varied. In each instance, the President's supporters would have had more votes than if weighted by population. However, the education and agriculture bills would still have been defeated and would have lost by greater margins than occurred in reality. The Urban Affairs bill would also have been turned down, but under the popular-vote weighting system it would

[13] Totals for the roll calls given in this analysis include pairs and positions as reported to the *Congressional Quarterly.*

TABLE 19. *Selected Roll-Call Votes, Actual and Weighted, in the 87th Congress*

House Resolutions	Actual Vote[a]	Weighted Vote[b]	
		By Population	By Popular Votes
URBAN AFFAIRS:			
For	156	145	170
Against	271	282	257
EDUCATION:			
For	179	143	161
Against	251	287	269
AGRICULTURE:			
For	212	183	191
Against	222	251	243
RULES COMMITTEE:			
For	219	211	222
Against	214	222	211

[a] Sources, Actual votes from *Congressional Quarterly Weekly Reports*, February 3, 1961, Rules; September 1, 1961, Education; February 23, 1962, Urban Affairs; and June 22, 1962, Agriculture. Roll calls have been adjusted to include pairs and announced positions as reported by *Congressional Quarterly*.

[b] Each congressman's votes is weighted by the population of his district according to the 1960 Census and by the popular votes he received in the 1960 election.

have had 170 supporters instead of the 156 who were actually mustered. And the Rules Committee proposal would have succeeded by three more votes than it received on the regular roll call.[14]

Does this exercise indicate that the conservatives in Congress are in fact underrepresented? For in six out of the eight weighted votes those opposing the Administration proposals had fewer votes on the actual roll calls than they did when votes were adjusted to take account of district populations and election results. If this is so, then it would appear that liberals have little to gain by reforms in the direc-

[14] On January 9, 1963, the House of Representatives once again voted to enlarge its Rules Committee. The actual and weighted votes on this measure were:

Vote	For	Against
Actual vote	236	196
Weighted vote (population)	234	198
Weighted vote (popular votes)	237	195

tion of equitable districting or even the curtailing of gerrymandering.[15] On the other hand, the use of weighted votes relied on existing congressmen and prevailing constituencies. If those favorable to more ambitious undertakings by the federal government believe that their cause will be aided by the equalizing of districts, then that hope must rely on the assumption that new districts will produce a new breed of congressman.[16] There is undoubtedly some validity to this expectation. But it would also be a mistake to overestimate the liberal propensities of American voters, especially when they cast their ballots for Congress. It is well-known that many Americans apply different standards to presidential and congressional aspirants—frequently supporting a liberal chief executive and simultaneously voting for a conservative representative.

It is therefore difficult to discover just what kind of policies the majority of Americans would like to see the Congress enact. In a way, the problem is irrelevant since representative government is intended as much to lead the public in new directions as it is to reflect current sentiments. But, in any event, the case for equal districts should be made on grounds transcending partisan programs. The real problem is not to secure more liberal or conservative legislation, but to give full representation to all Americans. How they will want to use their power, what kind of congressmen they will elect, what will be the ultimate legislative outcome—these are important questions, but they should not affect the overriding issue of equal votes for equal citizens.

[15] This may be why Republican Senator Barry Goldwater, an articulate conservative, expressed no worries over the possibility of redistricting: "I know there are those who say that the conservatives' political strength will be reduced if the cities gain more representation in the legislature. But I don't agree with that. I don't think it will make any change. There are proportionately just as many conservatives in the metropolitan as in the rural areas." Quoted in *ECHO*, newsletter of the Effective Citizens' Organization, April 1962, p. 2.

[16] It might also serve to weaken the seniority system by introducing more two-party competition into small rural districts. In the mid-1950's, 39 percent of the 38 House of Representatives committee chairmen and ranking minority members were from overrepresented districts, compared with 25 percent for the House as a whole.

5

The Prospect for the Sixties

THE NEW APPORTIONMENT of congressional seats was announced by the Bureau of the Census in mid-November of 1960. Of the 50 states, exactly half were informed that they would continue with their old delegations during the coming 10 years. These 25 states had gained in population between 1950 and 1960, but, for the most part, their rate of growth had simply kept in step with the national rate. Of the remaining 25 states, 9 would gain seats, and 16 would suffer losses in representation. In 1960, the membership of the House of Representatives stood at 437, accommodating the new congressmen from Alaska and Hawaii. But the new apportionment was based on 435 seats, Congress having decided to revert to its customary size.

The announcement of the 1960 Census results and the reapportionment of seats among the states provided an opportunity for redistricting action. States that had gained or lost population could alter the boundaries of districts so as to offer more equitable representation to their citizens. The Census Bureau gave the 1960 population figures for the old districts, so it was quite clear which constituencies were overrepresented and which were underrepresented. To what extent did the various states take advantage of this occasion to redistrict?

In seeking the answer to this question, only 413 of the 435 seats in the 88th Congress are being analyzed. The remaining 22 seats are at-large districts, thus giving every voter in the state a ballot of equal value in electing his congressmen. Five are representatives from small states having a single seat in Congress (Alaska, Delaware, Nevada, Vermont, and Wyoming). Four are from two states (Hawaii and New Mexico), each having two congressmen and electing both at large. Five are at-large representatives, elected in addition to the other members of their delegations, which have regular districts (Connecticut, Maryland, Michigan, Ohio, and Texas). And eight are congressmen from Alabama, all of whom were elected at large in 1962.

Several of these at-large seats are temporary expedients. The 1960 Census apportionment reduced Alabama's delegation from nine to eight members, but none of the nine incumbent congressmen expressed a willingness to retire. At first, the state legislature abolished the Birmingham district, distributing its residents among adjacent rural constituencies. This action, however, violated one of the "rules" of the redistricting game as it carved up a single county and passed out the pieces to nearby districts. A gubernatorial veto followed; hence, all nine representatives ran at large in the Democratic primary. The eight receiving the highest polls were then entered as the Democratic slate in the statewide general election and all were elected, becoming the Alabama congressional delegation.

Action and Inaction /

As a result of reapportionment, a state may lose or gain seats or retain the same number it had in the previous decade. A state that loses seats has to take some action; it cannot maintain the status quo simply because it has too many districts for too few congressmen. However, a state that gains seats, or carries over its preceding delegation intact, can do one of three things: (1) It can refuse to redraw its constituency lines, keeping districts unchanged, and taking care of any seats gained on an at-large basis. (2) It can partially redistrict, keeping some old seats and creating new ones out of the remaining territory. (3) It can draw up entirely new districts. These alternatives were exercised by various states after the 1960 apportionment, with differing consequences so far as the patterns of equitable representation were concerned.

States Which Did Not Redistrict

Eighteen states, containing 102 congressional districts, which neither gained nor lost seats following the 1960 Census, did not redistrict. Indeed, many of these states have had the same number of representatives for an extended period of years. For example, Georgia, Rhode Island, South Carolina, South Dakota, and Wisconsin had the same delegations in 1960 that they had in 1930. Colorado, Idaho, Louisiana, Montana, and Utah have the same strength now as in 1910. New Hampshire has had two congressmen since 1880.

When the legislatures of these 18 states convened in 1961, there was no imperative need to redistrict. In fact, there was at least one good reason not to do so: incumbent congressmen were accustomed to their old constituencies and would be very upset if they were shifted. Yet a failure to redistrict would mean, in many cases, that population movements within the state would not be reflected in a new distribution of seats. And this result, sometimes called a "silent gerrymander," is precisely what happened.

There are two ways to measure the inequities in representation among the congressional districts of a state. The first is simply to ask what proportion of the seats fall outside the 85 percent to 115 percent range of the population norm. This gives the number of districts that are either overrepresented or underrepresented. But such a figure, while useful, does not indicate whether the overrepresented and underrepresented districts are in marked deviation from the norm, or simply slightly over or under that standard. Therefore, the degree of inequity can be suggested by summing the deviations of all districts in a state and then taking the average.[1] For example, Colorado's four districts stood in 1960 at 112.6 percent, 149.1 percent, 93.6 percent, and 44.6 percent of the norm. Their deviations, in absolute terms, were 12.6 percent, 49.1 percent, 6.4 percent, and 55.4 percent, giving an average deviation of 30.9 percent.

Of the 102 districts in the 18 states, 59 or almost 58 percent were

---

[1] These indices are given in *Congressional Redistricting: Impact of the 1960 Census Reapportionment of House Seats*, Special Report of the Congressional Quarterly Service, September 28, 1962. The report, however, does not include computations of the average deviations for states or other groups of districts.

TABLE 20. *Eighteen States Which Neither Gained Nor Lost Congressional Seats and Did Not Redistrict After 1960*[a]

States	Number of Districts	Number of Inequitable Districts	Percentage of Inequitable Districts	Average District Deviation (Percent)
South Dakota	2	2	100.0	46.3
Utah	2	2	100.0	28.6
Idaho	2	2	100.0	22.9
Montana	2	2	100.0	18.7
Connecticut[b]	5	4	80.0	25.9
Oregon	4	3	75.0	20.0
Wisconsin	10	7	70.0	22.1
Oklahoma	6	4	66.7	27.1
Tennessee	9	6	66.7	23.2
Georgia	10	6	60.0	26.1
Indiana	11	6	54.5	19.4
Colorado	4	2	50.0	30.9
South Carolina	6	3	50.0	17.3
Louisiana	8	4	50.0	16.2
Virginia	10	4	40.0	14.5
Washington	7	2	28.6	8.6
New Hampshire	2	0	0	9.3
Rhode Island	2	0	0	7.0
1960 districts	102	59	57.8	21.4
1950 districts	102	44	43.6	15.7

[a] Source, *Congressional Redistricting: Impact of the 1960 Census Reapportionment of House Seats*, Special Report of Congressional Quarterly Service, September 28, 1962.
[b] Not including one at-large seat.

outside the equitable range, as shown in Table 20. In four of the states, all the districts were of inequitable proportions, and in each of 14 states, at least half of the seats were either overrepresented or underrepresented. The average deviations for the most part were quite serious, although not in direct correlation with the percentage of inequitable seats. The reason for the occasional lack of correlation is illustrated, again, in a state such as Colorado where the two seats outside the equitable range have a very high deviation from the norm. Thus, while Colorado ranks twelfth in proportion of inequitable districts, it stands second in average deviation.

The chief cause of these inequities is the prolonged period in virtually all of the states since the last redistricting. Despite the depopulation of rural areas and the growth of cities and suburbs, congressmen are distributed as if the clock had stopped in 1910 or 1930. Even the movements in the last decade, from 1950 to 1960, have contributed to the warped pattern of representation in these states. In 1950, 43.6 percent of their 102 districts were outside the equitable range and, by 1960, the figure had climbed to 57.8 percent. Thus, in 10 years, the percentage of seats becoming either overrepresented or underrepresented rose by 14.2 percent. Similarly, the average deviation for the 102 districts rose from 15.7 percent to 21.4 percent over the 10-year period.

There is evidence, then, that failure to gain or lose seats through reapportionment is not an excuse for failure to redistrict internally. Only in two states, New Hampshire and Rhode Island, have districts remained equitable in size despite the retention of old boundaries. Any step in the direction of equal representation will have to safeguard the rights of citizens living in states not now compelled by a change in delegation strength to redistrict. There will always be such states and among them will be a few that manage to keep in step with the national rate of growth for not one but several decades.

States Which Gained Seats but Did Not Redistrict

Four states—Maryland, Michigan, Ohio, and Texas—which received an additional congressman through the 1960 reapportionment nevertheless did not recast their districts so as to assimilate the new representative. The reason was internal disagreement, either within the legislature or between legislature and governor, that could not be resolved in time for the 1962 primaries and elections.[2] Hence, the new member was elected at large, either as an expedient or as a permanent fixture.

---

[2] For the story of what happened in three of these states, see the essays by Dwynal Pettengill (Maryland), Karl Lamb (Michigan), and Herbert Waltzer (Ohio) in Malcolm E. Jewell (ed.), *The Politics of Reapportionment* (Atherton Press, 1962).

These states should be considered separately from the preceding 18 since they received added representation because they grew at a faster rate than the country as a whole. The figures in Table 21 indicate that a state's overall growth is also an index of its internal population movements. The percentage of inequitable districts for these four states came in 1960 to 72.8 percent and the average district deviation was 29.8 percent. These figures are substantially higher than those for the 18 states which neither gained nor lost congressional seats. Moreover, the disparities accumulating during the preceding 10 years were also greater. In 1950, 55.7 percent of the 70 districts in the four states were of inequitable size; in 1960, the figure was 72.8 percent. This rise of 17.1 percent compares with a 14.2 percent increase in the 18 states not gaining representatives. And whereas the average deviation from the population norm for the first group of 102 districts rose by 5.7 percent between 1950 and 1960, it went up 9.9 percent for the group of 70 seats in four states.

What this adds up to is that the creation of an at-large seat in lieu of carving out a new congressional district conceals significant inequities which had been developing over the past decade. If states that do not either gain or lose representatives should be encouraged to redistrict decennially, there is an even stronger case for redistricting in

TABLE 21. *Four States Which Gained Congressional Seats but Did Not Redistrict After 1960*[a]

States	Number of Districts[b]	Number of Inequitable Districts	*Percentage of Inequitable Districts*	*Average District Deviation (Percent)*
Maryland	7	6	*85 7*	*44.9*
Texas	22	19	*81 4*	*34.0*
Michigan	18	13	*72 3*	*31.4*
Ohio	23	13	*56.6*	*21 4*
1960 districts	70	51	*72.8*	*29.8*
1950 districts	70	39	*55.7*	*19.9*

[a] *Congressional Redistricting, op. cit.*
[b] Not including at-large seats.

states that have gained one or more congressmen. For the latter states are clearly in the midst of a social and economic upheaval, and the forces attracting migrants from the outside are also causing their own residents to move from old homes to new locations in the state. If districts are perpetuated with out-of-date boundaries, then the number of citizens trapped in overrepresented and underrepresented constituencies is bound to grow to major proportions. Fortunately, there is some reason to believe that at least one or two of these four states will redistrict before 1970 arrives.

States Which Partially Redistricted

Of the states that gained or lost congressmen, 11 changed the districts in only a portion of their territory. The method of redistricting varied. For example, in five cases (Arizona, Arkansas, Iowa, Kentucky, and North Carolina), only a single district was held over from the preceding decade. New Jersey, on the other hand, retained 12 of its districts, and four of Mississippi's five districts were old ones that were carried over intact. As Table 22 shows, there were 182 districts in these states that took partial action, of which 50 seats were held over and 132 were new.

While it is true that a substantial majority of the districts in the 11 states were newly drawn, the contrast between the new seats and the holdovers is sharp. Of the 50 old districts, there were 54 percent outside the equitable range compared with 19.7 percent of the new seats. And the average deviation from population norm for the former group was 16.2 percent as against 10.5 percent for the latter.

Why were 50 districts, most of them of inequitable size, and many of them seriously so, permitted to remain? It seems that these 11 states were prepared to redistrict in 1961, yet all stopped short of doing the job in a thoroughgoing way. The answer takes two forms. In some cases, there were congressmen with small and congenial districts who had sufficient friends and influence in their state legislatures to ensure that their domains were not tampered with. In other cases, the held-over districts were large seats securely in opposition hands, and the legislature kept them unchanged so that excess votes would continue

TABLE 22. *Eleven States Which Gained or Lost Congressional Seats and Partially Redistricted After 1960*[a]

States	Number of Districts	Number of Inequitable Districts	Percentage of Inequitable Districts	Average District Deviation (Percent)
Arkansas	4	4	100.0	22.4
Arizona[b]	3	2	66.7	36.3
New Jersey[b]	15	9	60.0	34.8
Mississippi	5	3	60.0	19.4
Kentucky	7	4	57.2	28.9
Illinois	24	9	37.5	12.0
North Carolina	11	4	36.3	12.7
Pennsylvania	27	9	33.3	10.4
California[b]	38	9	23.6	11.4
New York	41	0	0	7.0
Iowa	7	0	0	5.1
Total	182	53	29.1	12.0
Summary:				
Heldover districts	50	27	54.0	16.2
New districts	132	26	19.7	10.5
Total districts	182	53	29.1	12.0

[a] Source, *Congressional Redistricting, op. cit.*
[b] Gained seats (all others lost).

to be accumulated in those constituencies.[3]

Taken as a whole, the 182 districts in the 11 partially redistricted states had a more equitable distribution than that encountered in the states that did not redistrict at all. This is true in terms of both the percentage of inequitable seats and the average district deviations from norms. Nevertheless, except for New York and Iowa, the partial action of these states led to the creation or perpetuation of inequitable seats and consequent discrimination against certain citizens.

States Which Completely Redistricted

Only nine states actually made adjustments in every one of their

[3] See Jewell, *The Politics of Reapportionment, ibid.*, the essays by David Minar (Illinois), Edward Cooke and William Keefe (Pennsylvania), Preston Edsall (North Carolina), Frank Way (California), and Gus Tyler and David Wells (New York).

constituencies' boundaries. One of these states (Florida), listed in Table 23, gained congressional representation; one (North Dakota)[4] experienced no change in the size of its delegation; and the remaining seven all lost seats in the 1960 reapportionment. What is most interesting is that Florida, the single state gaining congressmen, took redistrict-

TABLE 23. *Nine States Which Changed Every Congressional District After 1960*[a]

States	Number of Districts	Number of Inequitable Districts	*Percentage of Inequitable Districts*	*Average District Deviation (Percent)*
Florida	12	5	*41.6*	*19.2*
West Virginia	5	1	*20.0*	*12.0*
Kansas	5	1	*20.0*	*10.9*
Missouri	10	1	*10.0*	*8.5*
Nebraska	3	0	*0*	*9.3*
Minnesota	8	0	*0*	*7.7*
Massachusetts	12	0	*0*	*6.3*
North Dakota	2	0	*0*	*5.4*
Maine	2	0	*0*	*4.3*
Total districts	59	8	*13.6*	*10.4*

[a] Source, *Congressional Redistricting, op. cit.* Florida gained seats; North Dakota's delegation remained unchanged; and all other states lost seats.

ing as an opportunity to create seats varying greatly in size. One of Florida's seats is 160.3 percent of the state population norm and two others stand at 57.5 percent and 58.5 percent. Florida, however, is the exception to the rule. The other eight states redistricted quite equitably, with five having all of their districts in the range of 85 percent to 115 percent. The single inequitable seats in West Virginia, Kansas, and Missouri were not extreme deviations, standing respectively at 81.4 percent, 123.9 percent, and 117.3 percent of the norm. It might be noted in passing that these states which lost congressional strength were "good losers" in that they did not penalize some groups of citizens just

[4] North Dakota previously had two at-large congressmen and decided, in 1961, to create separate districts for each of them. This action, however, was not impelled by a gain or loss in the state's delegation.

because the state as a whole lost seats. Even with Florida included, only 13.6 percent of the seats in this group are inequitable, and the average deviation is the lowest so far encountered. Nevertheless, Florida's action does suggest that complete redistricting does not guarantee that an equitable distribution of a state's population will necessarily prevail.

Overall Trends in Redistricting

Of the 413 districts (excluding at-large seats) of the 88th Congress, 222 have retained the boundaries which existed before the 1960 Census. In other words, less than half the members of the House of Representatives are from newly created constituencies. There would be nothing wrong with this if the high proportion of heldover seats represented areas that had not experienced significant population changes. But the opposite is true. There can be no more glaring contrast than that between the proportion of inequitable districts and the average district deviations in the heldover districts, on the one hand, and the new districts, on the other. This shows up in Table 24. Whereas 61.8 percent of the heldover districts are of an inequitable size, only 17.8 percent of the new districts are. And while the average deviation of the group of heldover districts is 22.9 percent, that for the new group is 10.5 percent. The evidence indicates that if a state embarks on a complete redistricting program it is likely to carry out the enterprise in a comparatively equitable manner.[5] The problem is that so few states do a thoroughgoing job of redistricting after each Census.

In any case, of the 413 districts examined here, 41.4 percent were outside the equitable range. Moreover, 33 of the 42 states considered here had one or more overrepresented or underrepresented seats, contributing to greater or less degree to the total of 171 inequitable districts. Only nine states, with a total among them of 79 congressional seats, had all of their districts in the range of 85 percent to 115 percent. Quite clearly, then, the responsibility for the unequal representation of citizens in Congress lies with the state legislatures in virtually every section of the country. The nine exceptional states at least have shown

---

[5] This is not to say that there will be no gerrymandering in such states. Having observed the rule of equity as concerns district size, many legislatures will then proceed to manipulate boundaries for partisan advantage.

TABLE 24. *Summary of 413 Congressional Districts, Heldover and New, 88th Congress*[a]

Districts After 1960	Number of Districts	Number of Inequitable Districts	*Percentage of Inequitable Districts*	*Average District Deviation (Percent)*
HELDOVER DISTRICTS:				
In unredistricted states (no seats gained or lost)	102	59	*57.8*	*21.4*
In unredistricted states (seats gained)	70	51	*72.8*	*29.8*
Partially redistricted states	50	27	*54.0*	*16.2*
Total heldover districts	222	137	*61.8*	*22.9*
NEW DISTRICTS:				
In partially redistricted states	132	26	*19.7*	*10.5*
In completely redistricted states	59	8	*13.6*	*10.4*
Total new districts	191	34	*17.8*	*10.5*
All districts	413	171	*41.4*	*17.2*

[a] Source, *Congressional Redistricting, op. cit.* Excludes 22 at-large seats.

that equitable districts are a practical possibility. But the evidence so far is that few of their sister states have been moved to follow this example.

The figures for district size that have been cited here were taken from the 1960 Census reports. The Census count was taken in April 1960, but the first Congress to be based on this enumeration did not convene until January 1963. This means, of course, that all the calculations about equitable districts were over 30 months old, and thus out-of-date, by the time the House of Representatives sat down to business.[6] Thus, now there are probably considerably more than 171 inequi-

[6] The apportionment was also out-of-date. In April 1960, New York had a population of 16.8 million and, hence, received 41 congressmen; California's population was 15.7 million and it was given 38 representatives. But by January 1963, California apparently had climbed ahead of New York to become the largest state in the Union. Nevertheless, it would have fewer congressmen throughout the entire decade.

table seats. By the beginning of 1963, about half of the congressional districts probably were either overrepresented or underrepresented.

Unless they are compelled to do so, it is unlikely that many of the state legislatures will redistrict congressional seats between now and 1971. The consequence will be that the proportion of equitable districts in the House of Representatives will shrink with the passage of time, accompanied by a rise in the number of inequitable seats. The movement of population from rural areas and large cities to suburbs and medium-sized cities gives every indication of being as rapid during the sixties as during the fifties. It may, therefore, be suggestive to project the experience of the past decade into the one now upon us. As Table 25 shows, the 83rd Congress opened in 1953 with 64.4 percent of its seats in the equitable range, and by the time the 87th Congress closed in 1962 only 42.5 percent of the seats were of equitable proportions. In the 10-year period, then, 21.9 percent of the country's congressional districts became either overrepresented or underrepresented because of the exodus or arrival of inhabitants. Actually, the far greater rate of increase was among the group of overrepresented districts, which grew by 14.5 percent as opposed to 7.4 percent for the underrepresented seats. The reason for this asymmetry, as discussed earlier, is that while there are many points of departure in the current pattern of migration there are comparatively fewer ultimate destinations.

If Congress began the 83rd Congress with 64.4 percent of its districts of equitable size, it started the current 88th Congress with only 58.6 percent of its seats in that category. This is hardly an auspicious beginning, and it means that matters will be a good deal worse by the time the 92nd Congress adjourns in 1972, if present trends continue. Assuming no significant change, by that time almost two-thirds of the House of Representatives would be composed of congressmen coming from constituencies outside the equitable range. No fewer than 261 members of the 92nd Congress would be overrepresenting or underrepresenting the voters of their districts. This would be a substantial majority of the U. S. House of Representatives and the size of this projected group would stem largely from the reluctance of state legislatures to embark on complete redistricting programs at the outset of the current decade. Even if all districts had been within the equitable range at the opening of the 88th Congress, the passage of time and the

TABLE 25. *Congressional Representation: Past Experience and Future Projections*[a]

Districts	83rd Congress (1953–55)		87th Congress (1961–62)		88th Congress (1963–65)		Projected 92nd Congress (1971–72)	
	No.	Percent	No.	Percent	No.	Percent	No.	Percent
Total equitable	273	64.4	181	42.5	242	58.6	152	36.7
Total inequitable	151	35.6	245	57.5	171	41.4	261	63.3
Overrepresented	73	17.2	135	31.7	91	22.0	150	36.5
Underrepresented	78	18.4	110	25.8	80	19.4	111	26.8
Total districts	424	100.0	426	100.0	413	100.0	413	100.0

[a] All at large seats are omitted; and the 92nd Congress is assumed to have the same at-large seats as the 88th Congress.

movement of population would transfer about 90 seats to the inequitable class by 1972. But this was not the case, and the high proportion of overrepresented and underrepresented districts in evidence at the start of the 1960's can only mean an inauspicious outlook for the coming years.

In these projections it was assumed, of course, that no state would redistrict its congressional seats prior to the 1970 Census; actually, seven states embracing 63 seats in the House of Representatives all completed districting reforms in time for their 1964 elections. But before detailing the developments leading to these actions, it would be well to point to the interests that are at stake in the entire redistricting controversy. For the creation of equal-sized districts is not simply a technical question. While emotions are not so bitterly inflamed in this sphere as they are, say, over desegregation, redistricting entails a redistribution of power that is bound to be unwelcome in many quarters. Some attention, therefore, should be given to the conflicting interests in this arena. The issues are real, and if ideological overtones can be heard this is further indication of the strength of feeling that is frequently encountered.

Two Americas: Rural and Suburban

Experience with congressional districting during the fifties made clear that rural voters were overrepresented and that, for the most part, their extra seats were secured by depriving suburban citizens of equitable representation. Outside the South, large-city districts were roughly proportionate to population; and while mid-urban seats were underrepresented, they were far less so than the suburbs. The conflict, therefore, is essentially between two groups of Americans. On the one side are those living in small towns and rural areas; on the other are those inhabiting the fringes of large cities.

Actually, these two groups of Americans are minorities within the total population. According to the 1960 Census, there were approximately 36 million people in the districts classified as "rural" in the preceding chapter, and only 29 million in those under the "suburban" heading.[7] This may explain, in part at least, why congressional districting has not become a vivid national issue. Most Americans feel neither sufficiently underrepresented to become exercised over their muted legislative voice nor so overrepresented as to want to preserve an entrenched position of advantage. But among those who are most affected, many in varying degrees are conscious of the maldistribution of power and the benefits to be gained or lost by moves in the direction of equitable districting. That those who stand to gain or lose are minorities does not lessen the principles involved. Indeed, the theoretical question has always been one of "minority rights" and the extent to

---

[7] These are, of course, conservative estimates. In an early 1962 analysis of population composition, the *Congressional Quarterly,* February 2, 1962, counted 91 million Americans in districts it classified as "rural" and 33 million in those it called "suburban." In terms of population and regardless of district, there were 84 million rural Americans and 36 million suburbanites. The reason why these figures are so high is that the *Congressional Quarterly* breakdown of districts and population into urban-suburban-rural failed to make provision for what has been called here "mid-urban" America. Most of the Americans classified by the *Congressional Quarterly* as "rural" are actually "mid-urban," as are many of the suburbanites—especially those on the fringes of medium-sized cities. No hard and fast definitions are possible in this area, but the evidence still suggests that those who inhabit the countryside and suburbia are distinct minorities.

which they are to be safeguarded. In this instance, instead of the opposing force being "majority rule" as is usually the case, two minorities are posed against each other.

Rural America now has disproportionate legislative power and will not willingly part with its extra congressional seats. On its side is the simple possession of this advantage and its inclination to fight to preserve the status quo. Suburban Americans, on the other hand, would prefer more equitable representation in the Congress. When two minority groups clash, majority opinion may be the referee, but it is clear that a greater intensity of feeling on one side can contribute to the outcome. It is, therefore, in order to examine the ideology and interests of what has been called rural America. For these are the underlying currents in the debate over representation.[8]

The Case for Overrepresentation of Rural America

There is no denying that the population of rural America is on the decline. Approximately half of the country's 3,000 counties lost population between 1950 and 1960, and virtually all of these were in the countryside. The rural community has not been sharing in the prosperity that supposedly characterizes America's affluent society. The median family income for rural farm population was less than $3,000 per year in 1960, and that for rural nonfarm families was only a little more than $1,000 higher. Despite pleas and inducements, industry is not moving to the hinterland to the extent needed to blot up chronic underemployment, and the small businesses of small towns are suffering from declining patronage and the competition of national corporations. Young people are tending to leave—especially those with skills, education, and ambition. The outlook is hardly encouraging for this still-proud heartland of the nation.

Those who remain in rural America are aware that they have been losing status and power over the past several decades. They realize that

[8] It should be emphasized that the following paragraphs attempt to give a sympathetic rendering of the case for rural overrepresentation. The ultimate conclusion, as will be made clear, is that this case is not sufficiently persuasive to warrant the perpetuation of existing inequities. At the same time, I should add that I have lived for almost a decade in provincial America and have some personal familiarity with sentiment on this subject.

decisions once made locally are now handed down from Washington, New York, and other centers beyond their influence.[9] These decisions, often uniform and impersonal, seem to have little concern for the preservation of the rural and small-town way of life. Thus, there arises the conviction that if this way of life is to be safeguarded it can only be by political means. Economic power and social prestige may have gravitated to metropolitan America, but the rural areas can hold their own if they retain disproportionate influence in the political arena. This view was apparently accepted by Associate Justice John Marshall Harlan who, in his dissenting opinion in *Baker v. Carr,* said: "I would hardly think it unconstitutional if a state legislature's express reason for establishing or maintaining an electoral imbalance between its rural and urban population were to protect the state's agricultural interests from the sheer weight of numbers of those residing in the cities."[10]

The problem is not simply the "weight of numbers" said to characterize urban electorates. There is also the belief that the cities and suburbs have the economic and social resources to solve their own problems. Rural areas, in contrast, are said to be underprivileged, to need aid and support that can only be drawn from outside resources. And, to their inhabitants, it seems apparent that this help will not come voluntarily; hence, the need for additional legislative representation to ensure that rural America is not forgotten. The argument for added weight to the rural voice is that an increment of political power is required if the economic and social advantages of the cities and suburbs are to be balanced. From this point of view, the dictum of "one man, one vote" is appropriate when all sections of the country are equal in economic and social resources. But when one area is in a depressed state, it must have disproportionate political influence if its right to continued existence is to be guaranteed. The rural minority senses—no doubt, correctly—that its treatment at the hands of government would be far less generous had it not legislative power in excess of its numbers.

Those differing with the point of view of rural America might argue that there is a price for progress, that it is an abuse of the principle of minority rights to ask that one section of the community be shored

---

[9] See Arthur Vidich and Joseph Bensman, *Small Town in Mass Society* (Anchor Books, 1960).
[10] *Baker v. Carr,* 82 S. Ct. 691, 774 (1962).

up after it has outlived its social usefulness. For example, they might ask, why must the nation be taxed to purchase agricultural commodities that are not needed but nevertheless continue to be produced? A customary answer to this and similar questions is that the rural minority is a special minority, one deserving consideration that may not easily be claimed by others.

There is another reason why voters in rural areas and small towns believe they should have relatively more representatives than urban voters. This is the rural ideology which assumes that those who live on, or close to, the land are superior people. America has espoused the rhetoric of democracy, but there have always been occasions when the suggestion is made that some citizens are superior to others in character and virtue. Even Thomas Jefferson, for all his talk of human equality, could say:

> Those who labor in the earth are the chosen people of God, if ever He had a chosen people, whose breasts He has made His peculiar deposit for substantial and genuine virtue. . . . The mobs of great cities add just so much to the support of pure government, as sores do to the strength of the human body.[11]

It would appear that the Jeffersonian principle of majority rule and its corollary of equal votes for equal citizens applied only when and where the political constituency was comprised wholly of yeomen farmers. From this point of view, when citizens are of superior moral character, then all may be treated as equals. But, once a new and less virtuous element emerges in the population, lines of discrimination must be drawn and political power cannot be a function simply of numbers. Quantity, in this view, ought not to be permitted to outvote quality.

The assumption of the superior character of the rural life is by no means dead. Not many years ago an official of a national trade association could proclaim:

> Today the greatest threat to democratic institutions, to the republican form of government, and ultimately to freedom itself, lies in our big cities. They are populated for the most part with the mass-

---

[11] Quoted in Gordon E. Baker, *Rural vs. Urban Political Power* (Doubleday, 1955), p. 1.

man, devoid of intelligence, and devoid of civic responsibility. He talks only about rights and has no conception of responsibilities. He will vote for anyone who offers him something for nothing. Whether it be subway fares at half-price or public housing at one-third price. . . . Our one hope of survival as a free country is that rural and semi-rural areas still dominate most of the state legislatures through their representatives and still dominate the House of Representatives at Washington. Our best hope for the future is to keep it that way.[12]

Rural legislators seem willing to apply the same description to the suburbs as they do to the cities. Indeed, if the allocation of representation to suburban voters is any index, the countryside regards them with somewhat more disdain than it does those who reside in the cities. As noted earlier, state legislatures dominated by rural Republicans have been less than enthusiastic about giving a full political voice to their fellow Republicans in the suburbs. For the suburbs are, in many ways, more modern than the cities, and often appear no less willing to embark on extravagant programs of expenditure. At all events, there is little community of interest between rural areas and the suburbs, and

[12] Quoted in Lloyd M. Short, "States that Have Not Met their Constitutional Requirements," *Law and Contemporary Problems,* Vol. 17 (Spring 1952), p. 382. The celebration of rural virtue often emanates from urban-based quarters. Short also states (*ibid.,* p. 383) that Dean McHenry of the University of California once reported that in his state "privately-owned utilities, banks, insurance companies, and other concerns with crucial legislative programs have discovered some 'cow county' legislators more responsive to their demands and less committed to contrary points of view on key social and economic questions than are urban representatives." And, more recently, the Missouri Chamber of Commerce, in its magazine *Missouri Business* (quoted in *Nation's Business,* July 1962, p. 29), warned against the diminution of rural power: "Not only would the good business climate be adversely affected but the economic growth of the entire state could be curtailed as legislation for big city interests, such as some union leaders' proposals, sacrifices the interests of the state."

At the same time, there have been indications that large national corporations do not feel that their problems are understood by rural lawmakers. *Business Week,* September 22, 1962, p. 84, suggested after *Baker v. Carr* that more equitable districting "should mean a better business climate" for the large enterprise, and that "businessmen are starting to find that the results may be more beneficial than they expected." Some corporations have moved on from a fundamentalist approach to economic questions. When the Indiana legislature, with strong rural support, was considering a right-to-work bill in 1958, among the opponents were Seagram's Distilleries, Radio Corporation of America, and General Motors. There is reason to believe that larger companies no longer feel that rural political power is necessarily in their interest.

the former have few scruples about being overrepresented at the expense of the latter.

There are, then, two strands to the argument for disproportionate power for rural America. The first is that the countryside needs an added increment of votes if it is to be raised to a parity with sections of the nation that have been moving ahead at a more accelerated rate. If it is countered that there are other depressed groups in the population that might call for additional legislative strength on the same grounds, the reply is that rural America differs from all of them by virtue of its superior character and heritage. This second, ideological, strand is of interest, if only because it makes the plea for minority rights on a different plane. On the one hand, the rural minority sees itself as having been bypassed in terms of material prosperity and social influence and, therefore, asks for political power as a form of compensation. On the other hand, it regards itself as possessed of a moral excellence deserving power beyond its numbers, perhaps even to a degree where it may thwart measures initiated by groups less sterling in motive and quality.

It is difficult to argue with ideology, for discourse in this realm is based on interest and emotion rather than reason and logic. What can be said is that the sentiments expressed here, whether true or false by any objective evaluation, are deeply felt in the countryside. This depth of feeling means that a rearguard action inevitably will be fought in defense of rural overrepresentation on both the state and congressional levels. There will be dilatory tactics and judicial appeals—to be sure, not to the extent witnessed in the desegregation cases —in an attempt to preserve the status quo. For the stakes, whether material or ideological, are real; and if a minority feels it is being threatened it is difficult to argue it out of its own definition of reality.[13]

---

[13] Just how deep these currents of thought and feeling run throughout rural America is difficult to say. It is certainly true that those inhabiting the countryside have a higher standard of living than ever before—whether judged in terms of diet, education, or television sets. But contentment is always relative, and the gap between rural and metropolitan prosperity is significant. The most vocal opponents of redistricting are the rural politicians. Rural party organizations tend to be oligarchic, drawing their leaders from a selective group in the community. Moreover, citizens in small towns are usually deferential to those who control the organization, espe-

The Suburban Minority

Political experience in the United States seems to suggest that significant steps will not be taken to aid a minority unless the minority itself is exercised over its plight and its members are prepared to organize efforts for improving their condition. It has been indicated that suburbanites suffer from a greater degree of underrepresentation in the Congress than the other segments of the population. The question, however, is the extent to which this deprivation of influence is felt and the degree to which suburbanites are willing to expend energy to achieve redress.

The suburbs of America's large cities are, of course, symbolic of the nation's era of affluence. The median family income of the urban-fringe areas was over $7,000 in 1960, and almost a quarter of the families had incomes of over $10,000. In the Chicago suburbs, for example, the median family income was $8,388 and 34.8 percent of the families earned over $10,000.[14] These citizens are faring quite well under existing arrangements. Many of them have come up in the world, in both economic and social terms, and they can be counted as successful by prevailing standards. Suburban America has its problems, but they are the growing pains of a healthy child. The suburbs naturally have a political life and their residents turn out to vote in predictably high proportions. Nevertheless, there is a widespread attitude that most problems are personal in the sense that they can be solved by a raise in salary, a change of job, or rising to a new social circle. Whereas rural America tends to keep its eye fixed on Congress for agricultural price supports, a new military installation, or the dredging of a local river, most suburbs are relatively unconcerned with the federal government's role in their continued existence. For these reasons, plus the fact

---

cially as so many are one-party areas. The impression is gained that much of the talk about the rural way of life stems from party leaders who do not want to have their dominance threatened by the intrusion of new, and less deferential, elements in their districts. And such an eventuality would occur were small constituencies raised to an equitable size. Nevertheless, there is still reason to believe that the rhetoric of rural politicians in some measure reflects widespread sentiment in their parts of the country.

[14] U. S. Bureau of the Census, U. S. *Census of Population: 1960, General Social and Economic Characteristics, United States Summary*, Final Report PC(1)-1C (1962).

that suburban party organizations are only beginning to take on coherent form, comparatively little grumbling is heard from suburbanites over the fact that so many of them are crowded into a single congressional district. If this American minority is currently being deprived of its right to equal representation, the deprivation does not appear to be causing it untoward pain.

This does not mean that there are not notable exceptions to these generalizations. Suburban suits asking for redistricting along more equitable lines have been directed against the legislatures of several states, and others concerning congressional districts are bound to follow. Indeed, there need not be a groundswell of public opinion behind a complainant to ensure a decision on his behalf, and it may well be that the suburbs will receive more congressional seats despite the indifference of most of their residents to underrepresentation. After all, one of the tenets of democracy is that citizens should be given the blessings of equality whether they want them or not.

Equal Representation: Pro and Con

Legal principles and practical justice are not easily reconciled. The question may be raised as to who most needs the congressional seats at issue. The rural demand is not simply for equal representation, but for overrepresentation on the ground that the problems and character of its constituents call for a stronger than average voice in the chambers where laws are made. Spokesmen for the suburbs ask only for equal status with everyone else. From the rural point of view, therefore, the argument, is that rural America has a greater need for preserving its admittedly disproportionate share of power than suburban America has for even an equitable share. The rural claim is that changes in districts to provide equal representation for the suburbs would be a gratuitous gift to a section of the community already in a favored economic and social position; such a transfer of seats would be at the expense of a part of the country that could not easily absorb the loss.

One drawback to accepting this reasoning is that rural areas are only in a position to make their argument because they already possess more seats than they are entitled to as a minority. There are other underprivileged minority groups that could logically make claims for additional representation, but theirs would have to be for a change in the status quo rather than its preservation. It has been suggested that Negroes could use far more legislative influence than they now have, and their demand for extra seats would be no less reasonable than that now heard from the countryside.[15] Other deprived minorities such as migrant workers, the mentally ill, and the indigent aged might request added electoral weight, if only to reach a parity with their more fortunate neighbors. But if there are many minorities experiencing difficulties in our society, the assumption of the American political system has been that they must accept the principle of majority rule and try to persuade the majority of the merits of their case. Only the rural minority has been able to circumvent this principle. Its defense rests more on possession than on logic, and if there is to be a claim for the defense of minority rights it should be achieved by means other than distorting the districts of the House of Representatives.

The alleged superiority of rural Americans and their way of life, of course, cannot be either proved or disproved. It may be noted in passing that the small town merchant and the farmer of today are not exactly the aristocrats that the framers of the Constitution had in mind when they suggested added influence for people of quality. Nor is it clear that congressmen from rural areas embody more statesmanlike virtues than those elected by other kinds of constituencies. Even so, it must be reiterated that the House of Representatives has never served the function of an aristocratic chamber but, rather, has been to reflect the views of all Americans. In the final analysis, it is best to ignore all pretexts of superior character and a superior way of life, for there comes a point when such rhetoric is obviously a rationalization of vested interests which cannot be taken seriously.

The case for rural overrepresentation will continue to be made, if only because man is a rationalizing animal and feels compelled to give reasons whenever he seeks to gain or maintain a position of power. Instead of simply admitting that he likes things as they are because they redound to his benefit, he waxes philosophical and seeks to persuade others that such a state of affairs is in the general interest. If anything, these outpourings serve as an index of the intensity with which a group

[15] See "One Man, One Vote," report of a conference sponsored by the Twentieth Century Fund, September 1962, pp. 6-7.

feels attached to its advantageous position. And there is reason to believe that on the subject of political representation rural sentiment runs deep.

Nevertheless, the principle of equal votes for all Americans is the overriding consideration. The development of democratic institutions in this country has been undeviating in its movement in that direction. Complete equality will not be secured rapidly or without struggles in both legislative and judicial arenas. Those who seek to defend existing inequities are clearly on the defensive, and it is plain that the principle of equal representation in the nation's legislatures is closer to achievement than ever before.

Court and Congress

On June 20, 1962, a special three-man federal court handed down its decision in the first case dealing with the size of congressional districts.[16] James P. Wesberry, Jr., a resident of Atlanta and of Georgia's 5th Congressional District, sued his Governor, S. Ernest Vandiver, in an effort to obtain more equitable representation. Wesberry's district had a 1960 population of 823,680. The adjoining 9th District contained only 272,154 people, thus giving each of its residents a vote worth over three times that of Wesberry's. He, therefore, asked that the state be compelled to redraw all districts so that each was within 15 percent of the statewide norm of 394,312. His suit requested that this be done before the Democratic primary in September 1962, or that all congressional elections in the state be held on an at-large basis.

The case was dismissed. Two judges, Griffin Bell and Lewis Morgan, held that *Colegrove v. Green* was still a "controlling precedent" so far as congressional districts were concerned, and there were several reasons why the federal courts should not intervene on Wesberry's behalf. Judge Bell, writing for Judge Morgan and himself, stressed among other things that *Baker v. Carr* "was at pains to distinguish" the problem of state representation from any that might arise at the national level. He went on to give several reasons why the congressional districts present a different problem.

[16] *Wesberry v. Vandiver*, 206 F. Supp. 276 (1962).

First, Wesberry had raised "a political question involving a coordinate branch of the Federal government," and it was not clear that the judiciary had the power to interfere with the internal workings of its legislative counterpart. Second, Wesberry's request might well lead to at-large elections for Georgia congressmen in 1962 and the court was not prepared to "deprive others of the right to vote by district" simply because one citizen felt aggrieved. Third, Congress itself has the power to legislate on district size and has done so in the past; thus, Wesberry and others in similar straits might press for a new statute prescribing equitable districts and in that way "relief may be afforded by the United States Congress." Fourth, an earlier decision had required the Georgia legislature to reorganize its seats on more equitable lines and such a "fairly apportioned state legislature might well alleviate Congressional district disparity."[17]

Of the four points raised by Judge Bell, the first two may be treated together. Even before the *Colegrove* decision, federal courts not only assumed jurisdiction in cases where congressional districts were at issue but the action that was taken required at-large elections to be held in three states.[18] Thus, there is no constitutional barrier to prescribing conduct for "a coordinate branch of the federal government," and there is precedent for saying that prevailing congressional districts may no longer be used if they fail to pass certain tests. On the third point, it was not at all certain that the Congress was inclined to amend its own apportionment legislation, reinstating the 1911 requirement calling for equal populations. Apart from a few zealots on the subject, such as Representative Emanuel Celler of New York, all indications were that

---

[17] The case referred to is *Gray v. Sanders*, on which the Supreme Court heard argument on January 17, 1963.

[18] In a 1932 case, the Supreme Court sustained a suit brought by several Minnesota voters challenging a recent redrawing of the state's congressional districts, the major contention being that the redistricting act had been passed without the necessary participation of the governor and was therefore invalid. In upholding this contention, the Court enjoined the Minnesota Secretary of State from applying the new districts, and the 1932 election was subsequently held at large. *Smiley v. Holm*, 285 U. S. 355 (1932). The Court reached the same conclusion in two companion cases: *Carrol v. Becker*, 285 U. S. 380 (1932)—Missouri's representatives thus being elected at large, and *Koenig v. Flynn*, 285 U. S. 375 (1932)—resulting in the at-large election of two New York congressmen. For an analysis of these cases, see Anthony Lewis, "Legislative Apportionment and the Federal Courts," *Harvard Law Review*, Vol. 71 (April 1958), pp. 1057 ff.

most congressmen had very little interest in correcting district inequities. For one thing there were too many interests and sensitivities
that might be affected, not least those of senior lawmakers who represented safe and small seats. Michael Di Salle, then Governor of Ohio,
once had cause to remark, "Hell hath no fury like a Congressman
whose district is being tampered with."[19] Finally, there was no overpowering reason to believe that the Georgia legislature would correct
its own apportionment in so thoroughgoing a way that its reformed
membership·would be so composed and disposed to revise the state's
congressional districts in a similar manner. The halfhearted reappor-
tionments coming up from the states after *Baker v. Carr* were not
persuasive evidence that the legislatures were undergoing either
speedy or major alterations.

The Argument from Article I

On November 18th, 1963, the Supreme Court declared itself open for
hearing oral argument in the Georgia case, now retitled *Wesberry v.
Sanders* because Carl E. Sanders had succeeded S. Ernest Vandiver
as Governor.[20] Counsel for the Atlanta appellants suggested that legislative remedies seemed extremely remote: neither the Congress nor
the Georgia legislature were showing any great interest or alacrity in
producing statutory redress of districting inequities. Wesberry was
therefore appealing the lower court's decision which had said that the
federal judiciary had no jurisdiction in this area, and he asked for
immediate relief by order of the Supreme Court.

The constitutional grounds of Wesberry's argument were two: Article
I, Section 2, of the original Constitution, and the Fourteenth Amendment. The latter provision, requiring that all citizens be guaranteed
"equal protection of the laws," had been the mainstay in *Baker v. Carr.*
Clearly the states were as obliged to give their citizens equally
weighted congressional votes as they were to assign equitable ballots
for their own legislative elections. In the congressional case, however,
the Fourteenth Amendment guarantee would prove to be little more

[19] In Jewell, *The Politics of Reapportionment, op. cit.*, p. 187.
[20] *Wesberry v. Sanders,* 84 S. Ct. 526.

than an ancillary argument, for, while the states created the districts for House of Representatives elections, that chamber is itself a federal institution. Its character and composition are set forth in the Constitution of the United States, and the Congress itself is empowered to legislate on the size and shape of its own districts.

Wesberry's counsel, therefore, rested his case principally on Article I, Section 2. The important passage was the first part of paragraph 1: "The House of Representatives shall be composed of members chosen every second year by the people"—the critical words being, of course, "the people." What was requested was no less than an act of judicial legislation. Inasmuch as the Congress had failed to renew its old law requiring districts to be equal in size, the Supreme Court was being petitioned to take action in light of its companion branch's failure to keep its own house in order.

The Solicitor General, appearing as a Friend of the Court, reiterated Wesberry's emphasis on Article I. However, the government's approach was to ask that the procedure in *Baker v. Carr* be repeated— the case being returned to the lower courts for rehearing and settlement on its merits. This time the Justices were in no mood for such a delay, and the queries they put during oral argument suggested that they saw little to be gained in sending the matter back to Georgia for retrial. Even Justice Harlan, the chief dissenter in *Baker v. Carr*, wanted the issue of congressional districts to be resolved as soon as possible. "We're in it as much as we are," he said, "and I cannot see any reason for not deciding . . . the matter now."[21]

Less than three months later, on February 17th, 1964, the decision was handed down in *Wesberry v. Sanders*. The Court voted 6-to-3, deciding for the appellants. Justice Black wrote the majority opinion, in which he was joined by Chief Justice Warren and Justices Douglas, Brennan, White, and Goldberg. Justices Stewart, Clark, and Harlan dissented, the latter vigorously and at length.

Justice Black, writing for the majority, produced an essay in historical interpretation. Entering that realm of speculation so enticing to those who bear watch over the Constitution, he sought to answer the perennial question haunting so many other federal questions: What

[21] *New York Times*, November 19, 1963.

were the intentions of the Framers? Brought to bear witness to his opinion were the shades of George Mason, James Wilson, Elbridge Gerry, Alexander Hamilton, Hugh Williamson, James Madison, Luther Martin, Gunning Bedford, Roger Sherman, William Samuel Johnson, Alexander Martin, Edmund Randolph, Gouverneur Morris, and Benjamin Franklin. None of these had, in the course of the Philadelphia debates, actually come right out and said that the districts of the House of Representatives ought to embrace populations of approximately equal size. Indeed, the idea that a separate district might be created for each member of a state's congressional delegation had not even been mentioned at the Convention.

But the provision that Representatives would be chosen "by the people of the several states" meant, as Justice Black read it, that "as nearly as practicable one man's vote in a congressional election is to be worth as much as another's."[22] The basis of this conclusion is perforce a matter of deductive logic. If the Senate was to represent the *states* of the Union, its companion chamber was to represent the *people* of that Union. Citizens, like states, are sovereign units: they are neither divisible nor multipliable. Thus each person must be entitled to as much representation as enjoyed by any of his fellow citizens. The only way to achieve this end is by having equally populated districts, thus ensuring that every individual has an equal share in a congressman.

This, Justice Black suggested, is what the Framers must have meant. His reading of the debates supported no other conclusion: "One principle was uppermost in the minds of many delegates: that no matter where he lived, each voter should have a voice equal with that of every other in electing members of Congress."[23] Why else would the Framers have assigned congressmen to the states on the basis of their respective populations? If numbers of people determine the state-by-state distribution of Representatives, it follows that they count equally in the intrastate distribution of those lawmakers:

> While it may not be possible to draw congressional districts with mathematical precision, that is no excuse for ignoring our Constitu-

[22] *Wesberry v. Sanders, op. cit.,* p. 531.
[23] *Ibid.*

tion's plain objective of making equal representation for equal numbers of people the fundamental goal for the House of Representatives. That is the high standard of justice and common sense which the Founders set for us.[24]

Justice Harlan's dissent was also an exercise in constitutional interpretation. According to his reading of the available documents, members of the House of Representatives were simply allocated to the states, which would in turn arrange for their election in any way they saw fit. For example, there did not have to be multiple congressional districts in a state: an entire delegation could be elected on an at-large basis, as some delegations have been from time to time up to the present. What of the argument that Representatives were to be chosen by "the people"? This requirement, Harlan suggested, would be fulfilled so long as the ballot was not denied to any individuals or groups on a discriminatory basis. If Article I, Section 2, demanded that congressmen be popularly elected, that requirement did not necessarily imply that all votes cast had to be equal in value or weight.

What concerned Harlan most was the tenuous logic underpinning the majority's reading of the Convention debates and related sources. On the one hand Justice Black had pointed out that "in allocating congressmen the number assigned to each state should be determined solely by the number of the state's inhabitants." That, in itself, was true and beyond questioning. However, to leap from that proposition to the assertion that "equal representation in the House of equal numbers of people" called for districts of equal population was an unwarranted extrapolation. Justice Harlan sought to show that the men at Philadelphia were hardly committed to political equality as an abstract principle.[25] The "Great Compromise," calling a bicameral Congress into being, was designed to distribute legislative power as equitably as possible between the large and the small states. Article I,

[24] Ibid., p. 535.
[25] Ibid., p. 542, note 15. At this point in his argument Justice Harlan quoted the following from this study (the 1963 edition): "The assemblage at the Philadelphia Convention was by no means committed to popular government, and few of the delegates had sympathy for the habits or institutions of democracy. Indeed, most of them interpreted democracy as mob rule and assumed that equality of representation would permit the spokesmen for the common man to outvote the beleaguered deputies of the uncommon man." See above, pp. 7-8.

Section 2, was not written with any pretenses of popular democracy in mind:

> The appearance of support in that section derives from the Court's confusion of two issues: direct election of Representatives *within* the states and the apportionment of Representatives *among* the states. Those issues are distinct, and were separately treated in the Constitution. The fallacy of the Court's reasoning in this regard is illustrated by its slide, obscured by intervening discussion, from the intention of the delegates at the Philadelphia Convention "that in allocating Congressmen the number assigned to each state should be determined solely by the number of the state's inhabitants," to a "principle solemnly embodied in the Great Compromise—equal representation in the House of equal numbers of people." Although many, perhaps most, of them also believed generally . . . that within the states representation should be based on population, they did not surreptitiously slip their belief into the Constitution in the phrase "by the people," to be discovered 175 years later like a Shakespearian anagram.[26]

Justice Harlan, moreover, like Justice Frankfurter before him, was concerned over the Court's intervention in an area properly belonging to the legislative branch: "The unstated premise of the Court's conclusion quite obviously is that the Congress has not dealt, and the Court believes it will not deal, with the problem of Congressional apportionment in accordance with what the Court believes to be sound political principles."[27] But, Harlan went on, Congress had stated its views on equal districts—by its silence. The 1929 Reapportionment Act, successively renewed through 1960, made no mention at all of equality of population. This was all the more significant, for earlier apportionment laws had stated that districts had to be equal whereas such a provision was left out of the 1929 bill. Harlan drew attention to congressional intentions as evidenced in the legislative history of the 1929 Act: "The fact that such a provision was included in the bill as it was presented to the House, and was deleted by the House after debate . . . leaves no doubt that the omission was deliberate."[28] Indeed, bills designed to reinstate the equal-population requirement were periodically introduced in the intervening years but Congress did not see

[26] *Wesberry v. Sanders*, p. 540.
[27] *Ibid.*, p. 547.
[28] *Ibid.*, p. 548.

fit to take action on any of them. In the final analysis Harlan's concern was over what he considered to be judicial usurpation of a legislative function and with "the impropriety of the Court's wholehearted but heavy-footed entrance into the political arena."[29] His closing words echoed Justice Frankfurter's in *Baker v. Carr:*

> What is done today saps the political process. The promise of judicial intervention in matters of this sort cannot but encourage popular inertia in efforts of political reform through the political process, with the inevitable result that the process itself is weakened. By yielding to the demand for a judicial remedy in this instance, the Court in my view does a disservice both to itself and to the broader values of our system of government.[30]

First Steps

The full impact of *Wesberry v. Sanders* would not be felt until the 1966 congressional elections. The Court indicated that it did not expect redistricting to take place by November 1964: its decision, coming in February of 1964, did not allow sufficient time for states to rearrange primaries and adjust filing dates for a new series of district candidacies.[31] Filing deadlines for candidates are in March and April —or even earlier—in a majority of states, and the creation of new districts would produce more confusion than would be justified by immediate equalization. Just how many legislatures, reconvening in 1965, would undertake redistricting is not clear. The argument may arise that it is necessary to wait until 1971, when the Census figures for 1970 are available. A redistricting done in 1965 would have to be based on the 1960 statistics, since a mid-decade census, simply for apportionment purposes, would be far too expensive. Hence the courts may have to decide whether redistricting should proceed for the 1966 elec-

[29] *Ibid.,* p. 537, note 5.
[30] *Ibid.,* p. 551.
[31] On March 2, 1964, the Supreme Court upheld a lower court's decision declaring Texas' congressional districts unconstitutional. However, it reversed an order that all Representatives be elected on an at-large basis if an acceptable redistricting plan were not submitted in time for the 1964 election. Taking note of "the imminence of the forthcoming election" and "the operation of the election machinery of Texas," the Court postponed the deadline until 1966. See *Congressional Quarterly Weekly Report,* March 6, 1964, p. 474.

tions even though the population figures are a half decade old. The odds are that such action may be required, and demographers will no doubt testify that intrastate population movements are not at such an accelerated rate as to make the 1960 Census reports completely useless.

Georgia itself responded immediately: four days after the *Wesberry* decision its legislators redistricted the state's congressional seats—for the first time since 1931. The change was a thoroughgoing one, and all ten districts had their contours altered in one way or another. In particular, Wesberry's Fifth District, which had had a population of 823,680, was split into two new seats: one having 424,917 residents, the other 398,763. Georgia's districts for the 89th Congress will indeed be among the most equitable in the nation. Only two of the ten deviate by more than 15 percent from the state norm of 394,312, and the indexes for these two are 115.5 and 83.6, just a point or two off the margin of equity.[32] Whereas the average deviation of the old set of districts was 26.1 percent from the norm, the figure for the new districts is 9.9 percent.

Six other states redistricted in time for the 1964 congressional elections: Alabama, Colorado, Connecticut, Michigan, South Carolina, and Wisconsin. Actually Wisconsin redrew its electoral map in May of 1963, well before the *Wesberry* decision. And Alabama, which had elected its eight congressmen on an at-large basis in 1962, created individual districts for them in the late summer of 1964. (Federal courts also handed down decisions involving Texas and Maryland, ruling that while existing disparities in district size were too glaring the states could have until 1966 to redraw their constituency lines.)

The seven states which redistricted in 1963 and 1964 varied in the extent to which they approached an equitable standard. At one extreme was Michigan: during the 88th Congress 13 of its 18 districts were outside the 85 to 115 norm and the average deviation for all districts taken together was 31.4 percent. Its districts for the 89th Congress will present a totally different picture: all 19 of them (the at-large seat has been abolished) are well within the equitable range, and their average deviation is only 1.1 percent. Indeed, the population of the largest district is 417,174, that of the smallest, 403,263. This, needless to say,

[32] *Ibid.*, March 20, 1964, p. 569.

is an example of what a state can do if its legislature sets out to give effect to the principle of equal representation.

Colorado, Connecticut, and Wisconsin also redrew their maps so that none of their districts deviated from the state norm by more than 15 percent, although their average deviations were somewhat higher than Michigan's. The three southern states presented a somewhat different picture. As has been noted, two of Georgia's new districts are above or below the equitable range; this is also the case with two in Alabama. South Carolina's action amounted to no more than shifting a single county from one district to another, with the result that three of her six seats are still either too large or too small. The effect of this adjustment, for what it is worth, is that the average deviation for the South Carolina districts is now 14.7 percent instead of the previous 17.3.

These redistricting actions call for an updating of the statistics prepared for the 88th Congress (Table 24 above). In that summary a total of 171 of 413 districts were outside the equitable range, amounting to 41.4 percent of all House seats. The reforms made by the seven states in time for the 1964 congressional elections reduces the number of inequitable districts to 143; and the abolition of at-large seats in Alabama, Connecticut, and Michigan raises the total number of districts to 423. Thus the proportion of seats outside the 85 to 115 range will be 33.8 percent in the 89th Congress.[33] This must be considered progress in light of how soon after the *Wesberry* decision those reforms were carried out. There were, however, twenty-eight more states—in addition to Alabama, Georgia, and South Carolina—with districts outside the equitable range. Assuming that suits would be initiated in each of them during 1965 and 1966, it is clear that the courts would be ordering changes embracing the entire House of Representatives prior to the election and convening of the 90th Congress in January 1967.

Courts or Congress?

That the *Wesberry* decision had been an act of judicial legislation was beyond questioning. Congress had in the past enacted its own

[33] This calculation is based on the 1960 Census figures and does not take into account the further disparities in size caused by interstate and interdistrict movements of population between 1960 and 1966.

statutes dealing with the size of districts and had the authority to do so again whenever it pleased. Not surprisingly, the handing down of *Wesberry* drew a congressional response. Representative Emanuel Celler, chairman of the House Judiciary Committee, began conducting hearings on HR 2836 one week after the Georgia decision. This bill would require congressional districts to be compact, contiguous, and to vary no more than 15 percent from their state's norm. Bills similar to this one had, of course, been introduced by Celler during every session for the previous 15 years and full hearings had been held under his chairmanship as recently as 1959. This time, however, the intervention of the Supreme Court might arouse congressional interest, not least motivated by an attempt to recapture the jurisdiction and initiative regarded as the province of the legislative branch. Celler, in opening the hearings in February of 1964, struck just this note:

> The enactment of my proposal, providing for a 15 percent deviation above or below a state average, would be of assistance both to state legislatures and also to courts in deciding whether or not congressional districts meet Constitutional requirements. There can be no question about the Constitutional power of Congress to enact my proposal in this area. . . . Nor can there be any doubt that a legislative solution is far better than a judicial one in a field which is primarily legislative in nature and responsibility.[34]

Whatever the fate of HR 2836, the need for such legislation had become clear. Justice Harlan was right in warning against too-frequent judicial intervention in areas that are properly the responsibility of the Congress. While Supreme Court decisions upholding the civil rights and civil liberties of individuals deserve nothing but praise for their courage and dedication, there is the danger that that tribunal is over-extending itself. For the Court lacks a popular constituency, willing and able to rise to its defense in the political arena, and it is in danger of some day facing an outraged and powerful group that will curtail its jurisdiction in just the areas where it is needed most.

Moreover, courts can only order redress when litigation arises. If no one in Idaho, for example, brings suit against the state calling for redistricting, the courts are powerless to require such action in Idaho. And if there is no act of Congress specifying equal districts, the courts

[34] *Congressional Quarterly Weekly Report,* February 28, 1964, p. 407.

would have to intervene each and every time a new Census revealed inequitable disparities in district size anywhere in the country. Needless to say, a congressional statute would have to be enforced, hopefully by the Congress itself. Theoretically the House of Representatives could, at the opening of each session, deny admission to any member who was elected from a district outside the equitable range. In practice this would be too much to expect, and the result would have to be appeals to the courts in particular cases. An act of Congress, then, would not do away with judicial activity, but it would give the judges a specific statute—rather than the ambiguous words of Article I, Section 2—on which to base their decisions. Clearly this is to be desired.

Gerrymandering will persist, because all indications are that there is no way of doing away with it. To ask the courts to employ a test of "compactness" or to require that districts be "neutral" is to seek too fine a point. What has been shown is that if districts are equitable, then the advantages accruing to the gerrymandering party are not outrageous. It is only when there are significant variations in the size of districts that gerrymandering can produce serious cases of minority rule. With equal districts, the victor may get more than his share of the spoils—but not much more.

Equal representation, in sum, is best viewed as a question of civil rights. It must be guaranteed, as most civil rights are, under the "equal protection" clause of the Fourteenth Amendment, with such additional aid as can be secured from Article I of the original Constitution. As matters stand midway through the 1960's, several tens of millions of Americans are being deprived of their full voice at the polls and full representation in the Congress simply because they make their homes in communities that somehow have failed to secure political favor. While it is true that those who stand to lose by districting reform are themselves a minority group, the fact remains that overrepresentation of any section is had at the cost of underrepresenting another. The exaction of such a price is too much to ask at a time when the political equality of Americans has become a settled principle. With *Baker v. Carr, Wesberry v. Sanders,* and *Reynolds v. Sims,* the first steps have been taken. There will be further advances, for the goal is unambiguous and the path leading to it is clearly marked.

Bibliography

Baker, Gordon E., *The Politics of Reapportionment in Washington State*. New York: McGraw-Hill, 1960. 32 pp.
——. *Rural vs. Urban Political Power*. Garden City: Doubleday, 1955. 70 pp.
——. *State Constitutions: Reapportionment*. New York: National Municipal League, 1960. 70 pp.
Barclay, Thomas S., "The Reapportionment Struggle in California in 1948," *Western Political Quarterly*, Vol. 4, June 1951. Pp. 313-24.
Boyd, William J. D., ed. *Compendium on Legislative Apportionment*. Second Edition. New York: National Municipal League, 1962. Unpaged.
——. *Patterns of Apportionment*. New York: National Municipal League, 1962. 20 pp.
Carpenter, William S., *Democracy and Representation*. Princeton: Princeton University Press, 1925. 113 pp.
David, Paul T. and Eisenberg, Ralph, *Devaluation of the Urban and Suburban Vote*. Charlottesville: Bureau of Public Administration, University of Virginia, 1961. 68 pp.
——. *State Legislative Redistricting: Major Issues in the Wake of Judicial Decision*. Chicago: Public Administration Service, 1962. 34 pp.
de Grazia, Alfred, *Apportionment and Representative Government*. Washington, D.C.: American Enterprise Institute, 1963. 183 pp.
——. *Public and Republic*. New York: Knopf, 1951. 262 pp.
Dixon, Robert G., Jr., "Apportionment Standards and Judicial Power," *Notre Dame Lawyer*, Vol. 38, June 1963. Pp. 367-400.
——. "Legislative Apportionment and the Federal Constitution," *Law and Contemporary Problems*, Vol. 27, Summer 1962. Pp. 329-89.
Friedelbaum, Stanley, "*Baker v. Carr:* The New Doctrine of Judicial Intervention and Its Implications for American Federalism," *University of Chicago Law Review*, Vol. 29, Summer 1962. Pp. 673-698.
Friedman, Robert S., "Reapportionment Myth," *National Civic Review*, Vol. 49, April 1960. Pp. 184-88.
Havard, William C. and Beth, Loren P., *Representative Government and Reapportionment: A Case Study of Florida*. Gainesville: Public Administration Clearing Service, University of Florida, 1960. 77 pp.

Israel, Jerold, "On Charting a Course Through the Mathematical Quagmire: The Future of *Baker v. Carr*," *Michigan Law Review*, Vol. 61, November 1962. Pp. 107-146.

Jewell, Malcolm E., "Constitutional Provisions for State Legislative Apportionment," *Western Political Quarterly*, Vol. 8, June 1955. Pp. 271-79.

———, ed. *The Politics of Reapportionment*. New York: Atherton Press, 1962. 334 pp.

Klain, Maurice, "A New Look at the Constituencies: The Need for a Recount and a Reappraisal," *American Political Science Review*, Vol. 49, December 1955. Pp. 1105-19.

Kramer, Robert, ed., Symposium of 12 articles on "Legislative Apportionment," *Law and Contemporary Problems*, Vol. 17, Spring 1952. Pp. 253-469.

Larson, James E., *Reapportionment and the Courts*. Tuscaloosa: Bureau of Public Administration, University of Alabama, 1962. 92 pp.

Lewis, Anthony, "Legislative Apportionment and the Federal Courts," *Harvard Law Review*, Vol. 71, April 1958. Pp. 1057-98.

McCloskey, Robert G., "The Reapportionment Case," *Harvard Law Review*, Vol. 76, November 1962. Pp. 54-74.

McKay, Robert B., "The Federal Analogy and State Reapportionment Standards," *Notre Dame Lawyer*, Vol. 38, August 1963. Pp. 487-498.

———. *Reapportionment and the Federal Analogy*. New York: National Municipal League, 1962. 16 pp.

One Man, One Vote. Report of a Conference Sponsored by the Twentieth Century Fund. New York: Twentieth Century Fund, 1962. 20 pp.

Page, Thomas, *Legislative Apportionment in Kansas*. Lawrence: Bureau of Government Research, University of Kansas, 1952. 179 pp.

Silva, Ruth C., "Apportionment of the New York State Legislature," *American Political Science Review*, Vol. 55, December 1961. Pp. 870-81.

Steiner, Gilbert Y. and Gove, Samuel K., *The Legislature Redistricts Illinois*. Urbana: Institute of Government and Public Affairs, University of Illinois, 1956. 32 pp.

"Symposium on *Baker v. Carr*," *Yale Law Journal*, Vol. 72, November 1962. Pp. 7-106. And also the unsigned Note, "*Baker v. Carr* and Legislative Apportionments," *Ibid.*, April 1963. Pp. 968-1040.

Index

Index

Agricultural interests, 114, 115

Agriculture bill (HR 11222), 97-98

Alabama: Election of legislative majority, 44; elections at large, 101; judicial action reapportionment, 38; redistricting in (*1964*), 130-31; underrepresentation in, 87; value of votes in, 23, 45

Alaska, 3, 45, 81*n*, 100, 101

Apportionment (*see also* Redistricting): And state legislatures, 17-26, 30, 123; as judicial issue, 26-47, 122-33; attitude of Congress toward, 18-19, 48-50, 123, 128; based on population, 6-7, 36-50; colonial practices, 5; following *1960* census, 100-02; inequities in, 2, 79-99; process of, 48-78

Apportionment acts: *1842*, 48-49; *1872-1929*, 18-19, 49, 123, 128

Arizona, 3, 23, 45, 106, 107

Arkansas, 3, 23, 45, 50, 106, 107

At-large elections, 38, 81, 101, 104-05, 123

Atlanta, Ga., 87, 90*n*, 122

Baker, Gordon E., 72*n*, 116*n*

Baker v. Carr, 26-30, 31, 37-39, 124, 125, 129, 133; dissenting opinion, 4, 28-30, 115; representation in state legislatures, 20, 122; representation proportionate to population, 2, 16, 22, 31, 117*n*; state legislatures and apportionment, 17, 30, 124

Bell, Griffin, 122, 123

Bensman, Joseph, 115*n*

Bicameralism: In federal government, 3, 127; in states, 2, 31-35, 38-40

Biemiller, Andrew J., 21*n*,

Birmingham, Ala., 87, 90*n*, 101

Black, Hugo L., 19*n*, 125-27

Boyd, William J. D.., 22*n*, 26*n*, 32*n*, 35*n*, 72*n*

Brennan, William J., Jr., 27, 39, 125

Businessmen, attitude toward redistricting, 117*n*

California: Analysis of districts in, 80; attitude of businessmen, 117*n;* congres-sional elections (*1954*) 67*n*, (*1962*) 61, 65-68, 70, 73; growth, 110*n;* redistricting in, 107; representation of counties, 32, 40; value of votes in, 3, 23, 26, 45; votes v. representation, 51, 53-54

Carrol v. Becker, 123*n*

Celler, Emanuel, 49*n*, 123, 132

Census (*1960*), 100-04, 110, 113, 129-30, 131*n;* (*1970*), 129

Census Bureau, classification of districts, 88-89

Charleston, S.C., 12-13

Chicago, Ill., 87, 90, 119

Cities (*see also* Urban districts): Disparagement of, 116-17; representation of, 92, 94

Civil liberties, 36, 132

Civil rights, 35-36, 41-42, 132, 133

Clark, Tom C., 28, 31, 38*n*, 125

Colegrove, Kenneth, 17-20, 72

Colegrove v. Barrett, 19

Colegrove v. Green, 17-18, 26, 28, 122-23

Colonial apportionment practices, 5

Colorado, 3, 23, 38, 39, 41-42, 44-45, 102-03, 130-31

Compact constituencies, 74-77

Congress (*see also* House of Representatives; Senate): *83rd*, 111-12; *87th*, 96-98, 111-12; *88th*, 1, 100, 109-12, 130-31; *89th*, 47, 130-31; *92nd* (projected), 111-12; and the Supreme Court, 46, 122-33; apportionment acts, 18-19, 48-50, 123, 128; need for act requiring equitable districts, 132-33; need for bicameral, 3, 34, 127; party representation in, 50-54; regulation of elections, 9, 12-14, 18-19, 123, 125; representation of voters, 93-94, 98-99, 119; rural domination of, 117; "sense of Congress" resolution, 47

Congressional apportionment. See Apportionment.

Congressional districting (*see also* Congressional districts): Equal votes for equal citizens, 1-16, 99; inequality of,

139

44; value of votes in, 3, 22, 23, 45
Oklahoma City, 90n
"One man, one vote," 16, 46, 47, 115
Oregon, 3, 23, 45, 103
Overrepresented districts, 80-87, 92-95,
102-04, 111-12

Parties, political. See Political parties.
Pennsylvania: Apportionment in, 5, 11;
farmers in (1776), 10; redistricting in,
107; value of votes in, 3, 23, 45
Pettengill, Dwynal, 104n
Philadelphia, Pa., 11, 87
Philadelphia Convention, 7-10
Pinckney, Charles Cotesworth, 13, 14
Pinney v. Butterworth, 42n
Political cartography, 48-78
Political equality. See Representation,
equal.
Political parties (see also Democrats;
Republicans): Competition in dis-
tricts, 82-84, 91; representation in
Congress, 50-54; support in districts,
82, 86-88, 93-94
Population: Analysis of, 113; as meas-
ure of equitable districts, 74, 77, 126-
28; composition in districts, 82, 88-
95; movements of, 20, 111, 112; of
counties, 21-22; representation proportionate to, 2, 6-7, 16, 22, 31-32,
38-40, 43-44, 117, 130-31
"Proportionate representation," definition, 49n

Rayburn, Sam, 83
Reapportionment. See Apportionment.
Redistricting (see also Apportionment;
Congressional districting; Gerrymandering; Supreme Court): After 1960
census, 105-10; and state legislatures,
17-19, 22, 24, 31-35, 92, 109, 111,
129-31; attitude of businessmen,
117n; congressional action, 46-47,
129-31; overall trends, 109-12; rural
opposition to, 118n, 120
Reock, Ernest C., Jr., 75
Representation, equal, 1-16, 99, 122; and
Supreme Court, 26-28; as civil right,
35-36, 41-42, 133; Frankfurter and
Harlan re, 28-30, 127-29; in Michigan,
130-31; Justice Black re, 125-27;
Madison's views, 8-10; meaning of,
31-35; precedents, 4-16

Representation, unequal, 1-4, 12-14;
characteristics and consequences, 79-
99; in state legislatures, 20-26, 43-
46; measurement of, 102-03; of rural
districts, 20, 24-26, 33, 36, 39-40, 85-
86, 92, 95, 113-18, 120-22; of suburban districts, 20, 33, 85, 92, 113-14,
119-20; of urban districts, 20-21, 24-
25, 26, 36, 91-96, 113; responsibility
for, 109
Representative government, American
tradition of, 2, 4-14
Representatives, House of. See House of
Representatives.
Republicans: California, 65-67; comparison of popular vote and representation
in Congress, 51-54; Detroit, 76; Michigan, 68-70, 73; New York, 43, 63-65,
70, 76; representation of, 86-88, 95;
sources of strength, 93-94
Reynolds v. Sims, 2, 38, 39, 43, 46-47,
133
Rhode Island: Inaction after 1960 census, 102-04; size of districts, 73, 103;
value of votes in, 3, 23, 45
Rights, civil, 35-36, 41-42, 132, 133
Roberts, Chalmers, 54n
Roman v. Sincock, 38n
Rossiter, Clinton, 10n
Rules Committee (House Res. 127), 97-
98
Rural America, 113-18
Rural districts: Defined, 90-91; number
of, 88-89; party affiliation, 93-94
Rural electorate: Alleged superiority,
116-18, 121; attitude toward reappor-
tionment, 37; Colorado case, 41-42;
expectations from Congress, 119; in
South, 87; overrepresentation of, 20,
24-26, 33, 36, 39-40, 85-86, 92, 95,
113-18, 120-22; view of framers of
Constitution, 9-10, 12

Schmeckebier, Laurence F., 50n
Senate, U.S., 2-4, 6, 8, 15, 34, 39, 47
Seniority system, 99n
Seventeenth Amendment (Constitution),
15
Short, Lloyd M., 117n
Silva, Ruth, 96n
Slaves, constitutional provision re, 11
Smiley v. Holm, 123n

South, congressional districts in, 82, 84, 87, 96

South Carolina: Inaction after *1960* census, 102-03; redistricting in (*1964*), 130-31; unequal representation, 5, 8, 12-13; value of votes in, 3, 23, 45

South Dakota, 3, 23, 45, 102, 103

Standard of living: Rural America, 118*n;* suburbia, 119; variations, 82, 85-86

State constitutions, adoption of new in *1830's,* 14-15

State legislatures: And redistricting, 17-19, 22-24, 31-35, 92, 109; congressional interest in, 46-47, 129-31; "federal" system, 32-35, 39, 40; rural domination of, 39-40, 117; Supreme Court decisions re (*see* Baker v. Carr; Colegrove v. Green; Reynolds v. Sims, Wesberry v. Sanders); unequal representation in, 20-26, 43-46

States (*see also names of*): And the judiciary, 17-47; bicameralism in, 2, 31-35, 38-40; constitutional conventions, 12-14, 37; constitutions, 14-15; legislatures (*see* State legislatures); reaction to *1960* census, 100-10; redistricting in (*see* Redistricting); voting laws, 7-8

Stewart, Potter, 38*n,* 125

Suburban districts: Composition of, 82; defined, 89, 90; party affiliation, 93-95; rural attitude toward, 117-18; underrepresentation of, 20, 33, 85, 92, 113-14, 119-20

Supreme Court (*see also* Baker v. Carr; Colegrove v. Green; Reynolds v. Sims; Wesberry v. Sims): And Congress, 46, 122-33; redistricting in states, 19, 38-46

Swann v. Adams, 42*n*

Taylor, William L., 35

Tennessee: Inequitable districts in, 87, 103; judicial action on apportionment, 37; value of votes in, 2, 3, 23, 26-28, 30, 45

Texas: At-large election, 104-05; congressional representation, 81*n,* 87; districts in, 83, 101, 105; judicial action re, 129*n,* 130; value of votes in, 1, 3, 23, 45

Toledo, Ohio, 90

Truman, David, 74*n*

Tyler, Gus, 107*n*

Tyler, Texas, 89, 90

Underrepresented districts, 80-87, 92-95, 102-04, 111-12

Unicameral legislature, 32*n,* 34

Urban Affairs (House Res. 530), 97-98

Urban districts: Defined, 88-90; in South, 87; mid-urban, 91, 93-95, 113; party affiliation, 93-95; representation of, 20-21, 24-25, 26, 36, 91-96

Urban electorate: Disparagement of, 116-17; resources of, 115; view of framers of Constitution, 9-10, 12

Utah, 3, 23, 45, 102, 103

Vandiver, S. Ernest, 122

Vermont: At-large elections, 81, 101; value of votes in, 23, 26, 45

Vidich, Arthur, 115*n*

Virginia: Districts in, 49, 103; judicial action re apportionment, 38; unequal representation, 5, 8, 44; value of votes in, 3, 23, 45

Votes: Effective, 58-61; excess, 55-58, 64-67, 70, 71, 106; independent, 51, 53, 84; "one man, one vote," 16, 46, 47, 115; right to equality of (*see also* Representation, equal), 7, 9, 14, 16, 27-30, 99, 122; variations in value of (*see also* Representation, unequal), 1-4, 12-14, 23-26, 45, 79; versus representation, 51, 53-54; wasted, 57, 58, 64-67, 70

Waltzer, Herbert, 104*n*

Warren, Earl, 38-39, 40, 41, 43, 125

Washington (state), 3, 23, 42-45, 81*n,* 103

Wasted votes, 57, 58, 64-67, 70

Way, Frank, 107*n*

Wells, David, 107*n*

Wesberry, James P., Jr., 122-25

Wesberry v. Sanders, 2, 124-33

Wesberry v. Vandiver, 122*n*

West Virginia, 3, 23, 45, 50, 108

White, Byron R., 125

Willcox, Walter F., 50*n*

Williams v. Moss, 42*n*

Wisconsin, 3, 23, 45, 102-03, 130-31

WMCA v. Lorenzo, 38*n*

Women, right to vote, 15-16

Wyoming, 22, 23, 45, 81, 101